SUPREM

WATCH 2014

*Highlights of the 2013 Term and
Preview of the 2014 Term*

DAVID M. O'BRIEN
UNIVERSITY OF VIRGINIA

W · W · NORTON & COMPANY · NEW YORK · LONDON

W. W. Norton & Company has been independent since its founding in 1923, when William Warder Norton and Mary D. Herter Norton first published lectures delivered at the People's Institute, the adult education division of New York City's Cooper Union. The firm soon expanded its program beyond the Institute, publishing books by celebrated academics from America and abroad. By mid-century, the two major pillars of Norton's publishing program—trade books and college texts—were firmly established. In the 1950s, the Norton family transferred control of the company to its employees, and today—with a staff of four hundred and a comparable number of trade, college, and professional titles published each year—W. W. Norton & Company stands as the largest and oldest publishing house owned wholly by its employees.

Editor: Lisa Camner McKay
Editorial Assistant: Samantha Held
Marketing Manager: Erin Brown
Composition by Cathy Lombardi
Manufacturing by Sterling Pierce
Production Manager: Diana Spiegle

ISBN: 978-0-393-93781-7

W. W. Norton & Company, Inc., 500 Fifth Avenue, New York, NY 10110-0017
wwnorton.com

W. W. Norton & Company Ltd., Castle House, 75/76 Wells Street,
London W1T 3QT

1 2 3 4 5 6 7 8 9 0

CONTENTS

PREFACE

Supreme Court Watch 2014 examines the changes and decisions made during the Supreme Court's 2013 term. In addition to highlighting the major constitutional rulings in excerpts from leading cases, section-by-section introductions discuss other important decisions and analyze recent developments in various areas of constitutional law. The important cases that the Court has granted review and will decide in its 2014–2015 term are also previewed. To offer even more information in an efficient format, special boxes titled "The Development of Law" and "Inside the Court" are also included.

The favorable reception of previous editions of the *Watch* has been gratifying, and I hope that this twenty-fourth edition will further contribute to students' understanding of constitutional law, politics, and history, as well as to their appreciation for how the politics of constitutional interpretation turns on differing interpretations of constitutional politics and the role of the Supreme Court. I appreciate the expeditious assistance of Samantha Held and Candace B. Levy at W. W. Norton & Company.

D.M.O.
July 1, 2014

SUPREME COURT WATCH 2014

VOLUME ONE

2

LAW AND POLITICS IN THE SUPREME COURT: JURISDICTION AND DECISION-MAKING PROCESS

The October 2014 term marks Chief Justice Roberts's tenth term on the high bench. During his term, the Court has had an annual average of about 9,000 cases on its docket (ranging from 8,966 to 10,256 cases). The Court also continued the trend of granting oral arguments and plenary consideration to less than 1 percent of the cases on its docket. The Roberts Court heard on average less than 80 cases per term, or less than half of what the Court heard 30 years ago, when the entire docket was significantly smaller. As in the past, as indicated in the table below, the Court tended to grant cases in order to reverse the lower courts' rulings and to decide more statutory interpretation cases and those involving jurisdiction, practice, and procedure.

■ Inside the Court

The Court's Disposition of Appeals in the 2013–2014 Term

	AFFIRMED	REVERSED OR VACATED
First Circuit		4
Second Circuit	3	1
Third Circuit		1
Fourth Circuit	1	1
Fifth Circuit	1	6
Sixth Circuit	2	9
Seventh Circuit	2	2
Eighth Circuit		2
Ninth Circuit	2	10
Tenth Circuit	1	3
Eleventh Circuit		3
Federal Circuit	1	5
District of Columbia Circuit	2	2
Other Federal Courts		1
State Courts and Other	1	6
*Totals:	16	56

*Excludes cases decided on original jurisdiction or dismissed for lack of jurisdiction or dismissed as moot or improvidently granted and remanded.

B | The Court's Docket and Screening Cases

■ INSIDE THE COURT

The Business of the Supreme Court
in the 2013–2014 Term★

SUBJECT OF COURT OPINIONS	SUMMARY	PLENARY
Admiralty		
Antitrust		
Bankruptcy		3
Bill of Rights (other than rights of accused) and Equal Protection		7
Commerce Clause		
1. Constitutionality and construction of federal regulation		
2. Constitutionality of state regulation		
Common Law		
Miscellaneous Statutory Construction		22
Due process		
1. Economic interests		
2. Procedure and rights of accused	2	8
3. Substantive due process (noneconomic)		
Impairment of Contract and Just Compensation		
International Law, War, and Peace		1
Jurisdiction, Procedure, and Practice	2	11
Land Legislation		
Native Americans		1
Patents, Copyright, and Trademarks		5
Other Suits against the Government		6
Suits by States		
Taxation (federal and state)	1	3
Totals	5	67

★Note: The classification of cases is that of the author and necessarily invites differences of opinion as to the dominant issue in some cases. The table includes opinions in cases, whether decided summarily or given plenary consideration, but not cases summarily disposed of by simple orders, opinions dissenting from the denial of review, and those dismissing cases as improvidently granted.

H | *Opinion Days and Communicating Decisions*

■ INSIDE THE COURT

Opinion Writing during the 2013–2014 Term ★

OPINIONS	MAJORITY	CONCURRING	DISSENTING	SEPARATE	TOTALS
Per Curiam	5				5
Roberts	7	2	3		12
Scalia	8	9	5	1	23
Kennedy	8	1	1		10
Thomas	7	7	1		15
Ginsburg	7	4	5		16
Breyer	7	1	5	1	14
Alito	8	8	2	2	20
Sotomayor	8	6	5		19
Kagan	7		3		10
Totals	72	38	30	4	144

★Note that court opinions disposing of two or more companion cases are counted only once here. In addition, this table includes opinions in cases disposed of either summarily or upon plenary consideration but does not include cases summarily disposed of by simple orders, dismissed as improvidently granted, and concurring or dissenting opinions from the denial of *certiorari*. Note also that Justices Breyer and Kagan issued a joint dissenting opinion in *Hobby Lobby* and each are counted separately.

3

PRESIDENTIAL POWER, THE RULE OF LAW, AND FOREIGN AFFAIRS

B | *As Commander in Chief and in Foreign Affairs*

In its 2014–2015 term, in *Zivotofsky v. Kerry* (No. 13-638) the Court will consider the question of whether Congress may direct the secretary of state to list the birthplace of American citizens born in Jerusalem as Israel on their passports or whether that is unconstitutional because, in doing so, Congress would impermissibly infringe on the president's exclusive power to recognize foreign states. In its 2011–2012 term the Roberts Court evaded deciding whether Congress has the authority to dictate how the executive branch issues birth certificates for U.S. citizens born abroad. It did so in *M.B.Z. v. Clinton*, 132 U.S. 1421 (2012), when holding that lower courts erred in ruling that the controversy presented a nonjusticiable "political question" and remanding the case for consideration of the constitutionality of the statute in question. At issue is the validity of an over ten-year-old law in which Congress aimed to acknowledge Jerusalem as the capital of Israel, even though the U.S. government does not recognize it as part of Israel. After State Department officials refused to fill out a report on the foreign birth of a boy—Menachem Binyamin Zivotofsky, born in 2002 in a Jerusalem hospital—to show that his birthplace was "Israel," his parents sued, seeking to enforce the 2002 law that directed the State Department to do just that, when asked to do so by the parents.

4

The President as Chief Executive in Domestic Affairs

B | *Appointment and Removal Powers*

In a widely watched case on presidential power to make recess appointments, the Court held in *National Labor Relations Board v. Noel Canning*, 134 S.Ct. 2550 (2014) that President Obama exceeded his constitutional authority to make recess appointments when the Senate is out of session but still holds short *pro forma* sessions—sessions that mean the Senate is not formally adjourned even though no business is conducted—in order to deny recess appointments because of opposition in the Senate to confirmation of the president's nominees. The president has the power to make recess appointments when the Senate in not in session and thus bypass the requirement for the Senate's "advice and consent." In 2011 Republicans in the Senate held *pro forma* sessions, and in retaliation President Obama made several recess appointments to the NRLB, and his power to do so was challenged. Writing for the Court, Justice Breyer affirmed the president's power to make recess appointments when the Senate is in recess—regardless of whether the recess is intrasession or intersession—and the recess is of sufficient length, such as ten days but (as here) only a three-day *pro forma* session. Justice Breyer noted, on the one hand, that a ten-day rule was not absolute because emergencies might arise. But, on the other hand, he concluded that recess appointments were not permissible simply in response to "political opposition in the Senate [and that does] not qualify as an unusual circumstance." In a sharply critical concurring opinion read from the bench, Justice Scalia, joined by

Chief Justice Roberts and Justices Thomas and Alito, called the ten-day rule arbitrary and ahistorical. "These new rules have no basis whatsoever in the Constitution. They are just made up. . . . What the majority needs to sustain its judgment is an ambiguous text and a clear historical practice." But he charged, "What it has is clear text and an at-best-ambiguous historical practice."

7

THE STATES AND
AMERICAN FEDERALISM

A | *States' Power over Commerce and Regulation*

■ THE DEVELOPMENT OF LAW

Other Rulings on State Regulation in Alleged Conflict with Federal Legislation

CASE	VOTE	RULING
Northwest v. Ginsberg, 134 S.Ct. 1422 (2014)	9:0	The Airline Deregulation Act of 1978 preempts state law claims for breach of implied contract of good faith and fair dealing if it enlarges contractual obligations that the parties voluntarily adopted.
CYS Corp. v. Waldburger, 134 S.Ct. 2175 (2014)	7:2	The Comprehensive Environmental Response, Compensation, and Liability Act of 1980 preempts state statutes of limitations but not state statutes of repose that permit suits for injuries that may not become manifest until long after the statute of limitations has run out.

8

REPRESENTATIVE GOVERNMENT, VOTING RIGHTS, AND ELECTORAL POLITICS

B | Voting Rights and the Reapportionment Revolution

In its 2014–2015 term, the Court will again consider the matter of using race in legislative redistricting, though with a twist. Following the 1990 and 2000 censuses, Alabama reapportioned its legislative districts with the result that twenty-seven house districts and eight senate districts had majorities of African Americans, who tend to vote for Democrats. After the 2010 census the number of minority–majority districts remained the same, but this time the Republican-controlled legislature increased the number of minorities in most of those districts so that some house districts had minority populations as high of 76.8 percent and 75.2 percent in some senate districts. As a result, in other districts Republicans were favored to win over Democrats throughout the state. Black and Democratic groups challenged the new redistricting plan because it "necessarily increases the political segregation of African Americans and reduces their ability to influence the outcome of [elections in] legislative district[s] in the rest of the state." The combined cases granted and to be decided are *Alabama Legislative Black Caucus v. Alabama* and *Alabama Democratic Conference v. Alabama*.

C | *Campaigns and Elections*

A bare majority of the Roberts Court extended its controversial ruling in *Citizens United v. Federal Election Commission* (2010) (excerpted in Vol. 1), which held that the First Amendment protects corporations' and unions' direct expenditures to candidates for federal office and struck down limits on the amount of their campaign contributions. In *McCutcheon v. Federal Election Commission* (2014) (excerpted below), Chief Justice Roberts, joined by only a plurality, invalidated federal limits on the aggregate amount during a two-year election cycle that individuals' may contribute to candidates for federal office. Under the Federal Election Campaign Act of 1971, as amended by the Bipartisan Campaign Reform Act of 2002, a donor could contribute up to $5,200 to every member of Congress, up to a limit of $48,600, as well as contribute a total of $74,600 to political party committees. After *McCutcheon*, individuals may give $5,200 to every candidate for Congress of one party during a two-year election cycle, for a total of $2,433,600, along with $32,400 to each of the three federally recognized party committees and $10,000 to each of those party's fifty state committees, for a total of up to $1,194,400 in donations during a two-year election cycle. Notably, Justice Thomas, who provided the crucial fifth vote in a concurring opinion, would have gone farther and overturned *Buckley v. Valeo* (1976) (excerpted in Vol. 1) and *McConnell v. Federal Election Committee* (2003) (excerpted in Vol. 1), which had upheld those and other limitations on campaign contributions. Justice Breyer's dissent—defending the constitutionality of such campaign finance reforms over First Amendment objections—was joined by Justices Ginsburg, Sotomayor, and Kagan.

McCutcheon v. Federal Election Commission
134 S.Ct. 1434 (2014)

In the 2011–2012 election cycle, Shaun McCutcheon, an Alabama businessman, contributed to sixteen different Republican candidates for federal office, complying with the base limits on contributions for each. But, federal aggregate limits prevented him from contributing to twelve additional candidates and to a number of political action committees (PACs). McCutcheon and the Republican National Committee (RNC) filed a complaint before a three-judge federal district court, claiming that the two-year aggregate limits were unconstitutional under the First Amendment. That court denied their motion and concluded that the aggregate limits survived First Amendment strict scrutiny. McCutcheon and the RNC appealed that decision to the Court.

The district court's decision was reversed by a five to four vote. Chief Justice John Roberts delivered the opinion of the Court. Justice Thomas filed a concurring opinion. Justice Breyer's dissent was joined by Justices Ginsburg, Sotomayor, and Kagan.

☐ *CHIEF JUSTICE ROBERTS delivered the opinion of the Court, which Justices SCALIA, KENNEDY, and ALITO joined.*

The right to participate in democracy through political contributions is protected by the First Amendment, but that right is not absolute. Our cases have held that Congress may regulate campaign contributions to protect against corruption or the appearance of corruption. See, e.g., *Buckley v. Valeo*, 424 U.S. [424 U.S. 1] (1976) (*per curiam*). At the same time, we have made clear that Congress may not regulate contributions simply to reduce the amount of money in politics, or to restrict the political participation of some in order to enhance the relative influence of others. See, e.g., *Arizona Free Enterprise Club's Freedom Club PAC v. Bennett*, [131 S.Ct. 2806] (2011).

Money in politics may at times seem repugnant to some, but so too does much of what the First Amendment vigorously protects. If the First Amendment protects flag burning, funeral protests, and Nazi parades—despite the profound offense such spectacles cause—it surely protects political campaign speech despite popular opposition. . . .

In a series of cases over the past 40 years, we have spelled out how to draw the constitutional line between the permissible goal of avoiding corruption in the political process and the impermissible desire simply to limit political speech. We have said that government regulation may not target the general gratitude a candidate may feel toward those who support him or his allies, or the political access such support may afford. "Ingratiation and access . . . are not corruption." *Citizens United v. Federal Election Comm'n*, 558 U.S. 310 (2010). . . .

Any regulation must instead target what we have called "quid pro quo" corruption or its appearance. That Latin phrase captures the notion of a direct exchange of an official act for money. . . .

The statute at issue in this case imposes two types of limits on campaign contributions. The first, called base limits, restricts how much money a donor may contribute to a particular candidate or committee. The second, called aggregate limits, restricts how much money a donor may contribute in total to all candidates or committees. This case does not involve any challenge to the base limits, which we have previously upheld as serving the permissible objective of combatting corruption. The Government contends that the aggregate limits also serve that objective, by preventing circumvention of the base limits. We conclude, however, that the aggregate limits do little, if anything, to address that concern, while seriously restricting participation in the democratic process. The aggregate limits are therefore invalid under the First Amendment.

For the 2013–2014 election cycle, the base limits in the Federal Election Campaign Act of 1971 (FECA), as amended by the Bipartisan Campaign Reform Act of 2002 (BCRA), permit an individual to contribute up to $2,600 per election to a candidate ($5,200 total for the primary and general elections); $32,400 per year to a national party committee; $10,000 per year to a state or local party committee; and $5,000 per year to a political action committee, or "PAC." A national committee, state or local party committee, or multicandidate PAC may in turn contribute up to $5,000 per election to a candidate. . . .

For the 2013–2014 election cycle, the aggregate limits in BCRA permit an individual to contribute a total of $48,600 to federal candidates and a total of $74,600 to other political committees. Of that $74,600, only $48,600 may be contributed to state or local party committees and PACs, as opposed to national party committees. All told, an individual may contribute up to $123,200 to candidate and noncandidate committees during each two-year election cycle.

The base limits thus restrict how much money a donor may contribute to any particular candidate or committee; the aggregate limits have the effect of restricting how many candidates or committees the donor may support, to the extent permitted by the base limits. . . .

Buckley v. Valeo presented this Court with its first opportunity to evaluate the constitutionality of the original contribution and expenditure limits set forth in FECA. FECA imposed a $1,000 per election base limit on contributions from an individual to a federal candidate. It also imposed a $25,000 per year aggregate limit on all contributions from an individual to candidates or political committees. On the expenditures side, FECA imposed limits on both independent expenditures and candidates' overall campaign expenditures.

Buckley recognized that "contribution and expenditure limitations operate in an area of the most fundamental First Amendment activities." But it distinguished expenditure limits from contribution limits based on the degree to which each encroaches upon protected First Amendment interests. Expenditure limits, the Court explained, "necessarily reduce[d] the quantity of expression by restricting the number of issues discussed, the depth of their exploration, and the size of the audience reached." The Court thus subjected expenditure limits to "the exacting scrutiny applicable to limitations on core First Amendment rights of political expression." Under exacting scrutiny, the Government may regulate protected speech only if such regulation promotes a compelling interest and is the least restrictive means to further the articulated interest.

By contrast, the Court concluded that contribution limits impose a lesser restraint on political speech. . . . As a result, the Court . . . applied a lesser but still "rigorous standard of review." Under that standard, "[e]ven a 'significant interference' with protected rights of political association may be sustained if the State demonstrates a sufficiently important interest and employs means closely drawn to avoid unnecessary abridgement of associational freedoms."

The primary purpose of FECA was to limit *quid pro quo* corruption and its appearance; that purpose satisfied the requirement of a "sufficiently important" governmental interest. As for the "closely drawn" component, *Buckley* concluded that the $1,000 base limit "focuses precisely on the problem of large campaign contributions . . . while leaving persons free to engage in independent political expression, to associate actively through volunteering their services, and to assist to a limited but nonetheless substantial extent in supporting candidates and committees with financial resources." The Court therefore upheld the $1,000 base limit under the "closely drawn" test. . . .

The Court next separately considered an overbreadth challenge to the base limit. The challengers argued that the base limit was fatally overbroad because most large donors do not seek improper influence over legislators' actions. Although the Court accepted that premise, it nevertheless rejected the overbreadth challenge for two reasons: First, it was too "difficult to isolate suspect contributions" based on a contributor's subjective intent. Second, "Congress was justified in concluding that the interest in safeguarding against the appearance of impropriety requires that the opportunity for abuse inherent in the process of raising large monetary contributions be eliminated."

Finally, in one paragraph of its 139-page opinion, the Court turned to the $25,000 aggregate limit under FECA. . . . :

> The overall $25,000 ceiling does impose an ultimate restriction upon the number of candidates and committees with which an individual may associate himself by means of financial support. But this quite modest restraint upon protected political activity serves to prevent evasion of the $1,000 contribution limitation by a person who might otherwise contribute massive amounts of money to a particular candidate through the use of unearmarked contributions to political committees likely to contribute to that candidate, or huge contributions to the candidate's political party. The limited, additional restriction on associational freedom imposed by the overall ceiling is thus no more than a corollary of the basic individual contribution limitation that we have found to be constitutionally valid.

Buckley held that the Government's interest in preventing *quid pro quo* corruption or its appearance was "sufficiently important," [but] we have elsewhere stated that the same interest may properly be labeled "compelling," so that the interest would satisfy even strict scrutiny. . . .

Buckley treated the constitutionality of the $25,000 aggregate limit as contingent upon that limit's ability to prevent circumvention of the $1,000 base limit, describing the aggregate limit as "no more than a corollary" of the base limit. The Court determined that circumvention could occur when an individual legally contributes "massive amounts of money to a particular candidate through the use of unearmarked contributions" to entities that are themselves likely to contribute to the candidate. For that reason, the Court upheld the $25,000 aggregate limit.

Although *Buckley* provides some guidance, we think that its ultimate conclusion about the constitutionality of the aggregate limit in place under FECA does not control here. . . .

The First Amendment "is designed and intended to remove governmental restraints from the arena of public discussion, putting the decision as to what views shall be voiced largely into the hands of each of us, . . . in the belief that no other approach would comport with the premise of individual dignity and choice upon which our political system rests." *Cohen v. California*, 403 U.S. 15 (1971). As relevant here, the First Amendment safeguards an individual's right to participate in the public debate through political expression and political association. . . .

To put it in the simplest terms, the aggregate limits prohibit an individual from fully contributing to the primary and general election campaigns of ten or more candidates, even if all contributions fall within the base limits Congress views as adequate to protect against corruption. The individual may give up to $5,200 each to nine candidates, but the aggregate limits constitute an outright ban on further contributions to any other candidate (beyond the additional $1,800 that may be spent before reaching the $48,600 aggregate limit). At that point, the limits deny the individual all ability to exercise his expressive and associational rights by contributing to someone who will advocate for his policy preferences. A donor must limit the number of candidates he supports, and may have to choose which of several policy concerns he will advance—clear First Amendment harms that the dissent never acknowledges.

It is no answer to say that the individual can simply contribute less money to more people. To require one person to contribute at lower levels than others because he wants to support more candidates or causes is to impose a special burden on broader participation in the democratic process. And as we have recently admonished, the Government may not penalize an individual for "robustly exercis[ing]" his First Amendment rights. . . .

The dissent faults this focus on "the individual's right to engage in political speech," saying that it fails to take into account "the public's interest" in "collective speech." This "collective" interest is said to promote "a government where laws reflect the very thoughts, views, ideas, and sentiments, the expression of which the First Amendment protects."

But there are compelling reasons not to define the boundaries of the First Amendment by reference to such a generalized conception of the public good. First, the dissent's "collective speech" reflected in laws is of course the will of the majority, and plainly can include laws that restrict free speech. The whole point of the First Amendment is to afford individuals protection against such infringements. The First Amendment does not protect the government, even when the government purports to act through legislation reflecting "collective speech."

Second, the degree to which speech is protected cannot turn on a legislative or judicial determination that particular speech is useful to the democratic process. The First Amendment does not contemplate such "ad hoc balancing of relative social costs and benefits."

Third, our established First Amendment analysis already takes account of any "collective" interest that may justify restrictions on individual speech. Under that accepted analysis, such restrictions are measured against the asserted public interest (usually framed as an important or compelling governmental interest). . . .

With the significant First Amendment costs for individual citizens in mind, we turn to the governmental interests asserted in this case. This Court has identified only one legitimate governmental interest for restricting campaign finances: preventing corruption or the appearance of corruption. We have consistently rejected attempts to suppress campaign speech based on other legislative objectives. . . .

[W]hile preventing corruption or its appearance is a legitimate objective, Congress may target only a specific type of corruption—"*quid pro quo*" corruption. . . .

Spending large sums of money in connection with elections, but not in connection with an effort to control the exercise of an officeholder's official duties, does not give rise to such *quid pro quo* corruption. . . . And because the Government's interest in preventing the appearance of corruption is equally confined to the appearance of *quid pro quo* corruption, the Government may not seek to limit the appearance of mere influence or access. See *Citizens United*.

The dissent advocates a broader conception of corruption, and would apply the label to any individual contributions above limits deemed necessary to protect "collective speech." Thus, under the dissent's view, it is perfectly fine to contribute $5,200 to nine candidates but somehow corrupt to give the same amount to a tenth. . . .

The line between *quid pro quo* corruption and general influence may seem vague at times, but the distinction must be respected in order to safeguard basic First Amendment rights. In addition, "[i]n drawing that line, the First Amendment requires us to err on the side of protecting political speech rather than suppressing it." *Federal Election Comm'n v. Wisconsin Right to Life*, 551 U.S. 449 (2007).

The dissent laments that our opinion leaves only remnants of FECA and BCRA that are inadequate to combat corruption. Such rhetoric ignores the fact that we leave the base limits undisturbed. Those base limits remain the primary means of regulating campaign contributions—the obvious explanation for why the aggregate limits received a scant few sentences of attention in *Buckley*. . . .

As an initial matter, there is not the same risk of *quid pro quo* corruption or its appearance when money flows through independent actors to a candidate, as when a donor contributes to a candidate directly. When an individual contributes to a candidate, a party committee, or a PAC, the individual must by law cede control over the funds. The Government admits that if the funds are subsequently rerouted to a particular candidate, such action occurs at the initial recipient's discretion—not the donor's. As a consequence, the chain of attribution grows longer, and any credit must be shared among the various actors along the way. For those reasons, the risk of *quid pro quo* corruption is generally applicable only to "the narrow category of money gifts that are directed, in some manner, to a candidate or officeholder." . . .

Buckley upheld aggregate limits only on the ground that they prevented channeling money to candidates beyond the base limits. The absence of such a prospect today belies the Government's asserted objective of preventing corruption or its appearance. The improbability of circumvention indicates that the aggregate limits instead further the impermissible objective of simply limiting the amount of money in political campaigns.

Quite apart from the foregoing, the aggregate limits violate the First Amendment because they are not "closely drawn to avoid unnecessary abridgment of associational freedoms." *Buckley*. . . . Here, because the statute is poorly tailored to the Government's interest in preventing circumvention of the base limits, it impermissibly restricts participation in the political process. . . .

Importantly, there are multiple alternatives available to Congress that would serve the Government's anticircumvention interest, while avoiding "unnecessary abridgment" of First Amendment rights.

The most obvious might involve targeted restrictions on transfers among candidates and political committees. There are currently no such limits on transfers among party committees and from candidates to party committees. . . .

One possible option for restricting transfers would be to require contributions above the current aggregate limits to be deposited into segregated, nontransferable accounts and spent only by their recipients. . . .

Other alternatives might focus on earmarking. Many of the scenarios that the Government and the dissent hypothesize involve at least implicit agreements to circumvent the base limits—agreements that are already prohibited by the earmarking rules. The FEC might strengthen those rules further by, for example, defining how many candidates a PAC must support in order to ensure that "a substantial portion" of a donor's contribution is not rerouted to a certain candidate. Congress might also consider a modified version of the aggregate limits, such as one that prohibits donors who have contributed the current maximum sums from further contributing to political committees that have indicated they will support candidates to whom the donor has already contributed. To be sure, the existing earmarking provision does not define "the outer limit of acceptable tailoring." But tighter rules could have a significant effect, especially when adopted in concert with other measures.

We do not mean to opine on the validity of any particular proposal. The point is that there are numerous alternative approaches available to Congress to prevent circumvention of the base limits. . . .

For the past 40 years, our campaign finance jurisprudence has focused on the need to preserve authority for the Government to combat corruption, without at the same time compromising the political responsiveness at the heart of the democratic process, or allowing the Government to favor some participants in that process over others. As Edmund Burke explained in his famous speech to the electors of Bristol, a representative owes constituents the exercise of his "mature judgment," but judgment informed by "the strictest union, the closest correspondence, and the most unreserved communication with his constituents." Constituents have the right to support candidates who share their views and concerns. Representatives are not to follow constituent orders, but can be expected to be cognizant of and responsive to those concerns. Such responsiveness is key to the very concept of self-governance through elected officials.

The Government has a strong interest, no less critical to our democratic system, in combatting corruption and its appearance. We have, however, held that this interest must be limited to a specific kind of corruption—*quid pro quo* corruption—in order to ensure that the Government's efforts do not have the effect of restricting the First Amendment right of citizens to choose who shall govern them. For the reasons set forth, we conclude that the aggregate limits on contributions do not further the only governmental interest this Court accepted as legitimate in *Buckley*. They instead intrude without justification on a citizen's ability to exercise "the most fundamental First Amendment activities."

The judgment of the District Court is reversed, and the case is remanded for further proceedings.

☐ *Justice THOMAS, concurring in the judgment.*

I adhere to the view that this Court's decision in *Buckley v. Valeo* denigrates core First Amendment speech and should be overruled. Contributions to political campaigns, no less than direct expenditures, "generate essential political speech" by fostering discussion of public issues and candidate qualifications. . . .

As I have explained before, "[t]he analytic foundation of *Buckley* . . . was tenuous from the very beginning and has only continued to erode in the intervening years." To justify a lesser standard of review for contribution limits, *Buckley* relied on the premise that contributions are different in kind from direct expenditures. None of the Court's bases for that premise withstands careful review. The linchpin of the Court's analysis was its assertion that "[w]hile contributions may result in political expression if spent by a candidate or an association to present views to the voters, the transformation of contributions into political debate involves speech by someone other than the contributor." But that "'speech by proxy'" rationale quickly breaks down, given that "[e]ven in the case of a direct expenditure, there is usually some go-between that facilitates the dissemination of the spender's message—for instance, an advertising agency or a television station." Moreover, we have since rejected the "'proxy speech'" approach as affording insufficient First Amendment protection to "the voices of those of modest means as opposed to those sufficiently wealthy to be able to buy expensive media ads with their own resources." *Federal Election Comm'n v. National Conservative Political Action Comm.* . . .

Among the Government's justifications for the aggregate limits set forth in the Bipartisan Campaign Reform Act of 2002 (BCRA) is that "an individual can engage in the 'symbolic act of contributing' to as many entities as he wishes." That is, the Government contends that aggregate limits are constitutional as long as an individual can still contribute some token amount (a dime, for example) to each of his preferred candidates. The plurality, quite correctly, rejects that argument, noting that "[i]t is no answer to say that the individual can simply contribute less money to more people."

What the plurality does not recognize is that the same logic also defeats the reasoning from *Buckley* on which the plurality purports to rely. Under the plurality's analysis, limiting the amount of money a person may give to a candidate does impose a direct restraint on his political communication; if it did not, the aggregate limits at issue here would not create "a special burden on broader participation in the democratic process." I am wholly in agreement with the plurality's conclusion on this point: "[T]he Government may not penalize an individual for 'robustly exercis[ing]' his First Amendment rights." I regret only that the plurality does not acknowledge that today's decision, although purporting not to overrule *Buckley*, continues to chip away at its footings.

In sum, what remains of *Buckley* is a rule without a rationale. Contributions and expenditures are simply "two sides of the same First Amendment coin," and our efforts to distinguish the two have produced mere "word games" rather than any cognizable principle of constitutional law. For that reason, I would overrule *Buckley* and subject the aggregate limits in BCRA to strict scrutiny, which they would surely fail. . . .

☐ *Justice BREYER, with whom Justice GINSBURG, Justice SOTOMAYOR, and Justice KAGAN join, dissenting.*

Nearly 40 years ago in *Buckley v. Valeo* this Court considered the constitutionality of laws that imposed limits upon the overall amount a single person can contribute to all federal candidates, political parties, and committees taken together. The Court held that those limits did not violate the Constitution.

The *Buckley* Court focused upon the same problem that concerns the Court today, [limits on aggregate campaign contributions]. . . . Today a majority of the Court overrules [*Buckley's*] holding. It is wrong to do so. Its conclusion rests upon its own, not a record-based, view of the facts. Its legal analysis is faulty: It misconstrues the nature of the competing constitutional interests at stake. It understates the importance of protecting the political integrity of our governmental institutions. It creates a loophole that will allow a single individual to contribute millions of dollars to a political party or to a candidate's campaign. Taken together with *Citizens United*, today's decision eviscerates our Nation's campaign finance laws, leaving a remnant incapable of dealing with the grave problems of democratic legitimacy that those laws were intended to resolve.

The plurality concludes that the aggregate contribution limits " 'unnecessar[ily] abridg[e]' " First Amendment rights. . . . The plurality's conclusion rests upon three separate but related claims. Each is fatally flawed. First, the plurality says that given the base limits on contributions to candidates and political committees, aggregate limits do not further any independent governmental objective worthy of protection. And that is because, given the base limits, "[s]pending large sums of money in connection with elections" does not "give rise to . . . corruption." In making this argument, the plurality relies heavily upon a narrow definition of "corruption" that excludes efforts to obtain " 'influence over or access to' elected officials or political parties."

Second, the plurality assesses the instrumental objective of the aggregate limits, namely, safeguarding the base limits. It finds that they "do not serve that function in any meaningful way." That is because, even without the aggregate limits, the possibilities for circumventing the base limits are "implausible" and "divorced from reality."

Third, the plurality says the aggregate limits are not a "'reasonable'" policy tool. Rather, they are "poorly tailored to the Government's interest in preventing circumvention of the base limits." The plurality imagines several alternative regulations that it says might just as effectively thwart circumvention. Accordingly, it finds, the aggregate caps are out of "'proportion to the [anticorruption] interest served.'"

The plurality's first claim—that large aggregate contributions do not "give rise" to "corruption"—is plausible only because the plurality defines "corruption" too narrowly. The plurality describes the constitutionally permissible objective of campaign finance regulation as follows: "Congress may target only a specific type of corruption—'quid pro quo' corruption." It then defines *quid pro quo* corruption to mean no more than "a direct exchange of an official act for money"—an act akin to bribery. It adds specifically that corruption does not include efforts to "garner 'influence over or access to' elected officials or political parties." . . .

This critically important definition of "corruption" is inconsistent with the Court's prior case law (with the possible exception of *Citizens United*, as I will explain below). It is virtually impossible to reconcile with this Court's decision in *McConnell* [*v. Federal Election Commission*, 540 U.S. 93 (2003)], upholding the Bipartisan Campaign Reform Act of 2002 (BCRA). And it misunderstands the constitutional importance of the interests at stake. In fact, constitutional interests—indeed, First Amendment interests—lie on both sides of the legal equation.

In reality, as the history of campaign finance reform shows and as our earlier cases on the subject have recognized, the anticorruption interest that drives Congress to regulate campaign contributions is a far broader, more important interest than the plurality acknowledges. It is an interest in maintaining the integrity of our public governmental institutions. And it is an interest rooted in the Constitution and in the First Amendment itself.

Consider at least one reason why the First Amendment protects political speech. Speech does not exist in a vacuum. Rather, political communication seeks to secure government action. A politically oriented "marketplace of ideas" seeks to form a public opinion that can and will influence elected representatives. . . .

The Framers had good reason to emphasize this same connection between political speech and governmental action. An influential 18th-century continental philosopher had argued that in a representative democracy, the people lose control of their representatives between elections, during which interim periods they were "in chains." J. Rousseau, *An Inquiry Into the Nature of the Social Contract* (transl. 1791).

The Framers responded to this criticism both by requiring frequent elections to federal office, and by enacting a First Amendment that would facilitate a "chain of communication between the people, and those, to whom they have committed the exercise of the powers of government." J. Wilson, *Commentaries on the Constitution of the United States of America* (1792). This "chain" would establish the necessary "communion of interests and sympathy of sentiments" between the people and their representatives, so that public opinion could be channeled into effective governmental action. *The Federalist* No. 57. Accordingly, the First Amendment advances not only the individual's right to engage in political speech, but also the public's interest in preserving a democratic order in which collective speech matters.

What has this to do with corruption? It has everything to do with corruption. Corruption breaks the constitutionally necessary "chain of communication" between the people and their representatives. It derails the essential speech-to-government-action tie. Where enough money calls the tune, the general public will not be heard. Insofar as corruption cuts the link between political thought and political action, a free marketplace of political ideas loses its point. That is one reason why the Court has stressed the constitutional importance of Congress' concern that a few large donations not drown out the voices of the many. . . .

The "appearance of corruption" can make matters worse. It can lead the public to believe that its efforts to communicate with its representatives or to help sway public opinion have little purpose. And a cynical public can lose interest in political participation altogether. . . .

The upshot is that the interests the Court has long described as preventing "corruption" or the "appearance of corruption" are more than ordinary factors to be weighed against the constitutional right to political speech. Rather, they are interests rooted in the First Amendment itself. They are rooted in the constitutional effort to create a democracy responsive to the people—a government where laws reflect the very thoughts, views, ideas, and sentiments, the expression of which the First Amendment protects. Given that end, we can and should understand campaign finance laws as resting upon a broader and more significant constitutional rationale than the plurality's limited definition of "corruption" suggests. We should see these laws as seeking in significant part to strengthen, rather than weaken, the First Amendment. To say this is not to deny the potential for conflict between (1) the need to permit contributions that pay for the diffusion of ideas, and (2) the need to limit payments in order to help maintain the integrity of the electoral process. But that conflict takes place within, not outside, the First Amendment's boundaries. . . .

[I]n *McConnell*, this Court considered the constitutionality of the Bipartisan Campaign Reform Act of 2002, an Act that set new limits on "soft money" contributions to political parties. "Soft money" referred to funds that, prior to BCRA, were freely donated to parties for activities other than directly helping elect a federal candidate—activities such as voter registration, "get out the vote" drives, and advertising that did not expressly advocate a federal candidate's election or defeat. BCRA imposed a new ban on soft money contributions to national party committees, and greatly curtailed them in respect to state and local parties.

The Court in *McConnell* upheld these new contribution restrictions under the First Amendment for the very reason the plurality today discounts or ignores. Namely, the Court found they thwarted a significant risk of corruption—understood not as *quid pro quo* bribery, but as privileged access to and pernicious influence upon elected representatives.

In reaching its conclusion in *McConnell*, the Court relied upon a vast record compiled in the District Court. . . . There was an indisputable link between generous political donations and opportunity after opportunity to make one's case directly to a Member of Congress. . . .

The plurality's use of *Citizens United*'s narrow definition of corruption here, however, is a different matter. That use does not come accompanied with a limiting context (independent expenditures by corporations and unions) or limiting language. It applies to the whole of campaign finance regulation. And, as I have pointed out, it is flatly inconsistent with the broader definition of corruption upon which *McConnell*'s holding depends.

So: Does the Court intend today to overrule *McConnell*? Or does it intend to leave McConnell and BCRA in place? The plurality says the latter. But how does the plurality explain its rejection of the broader definition of corruption, upon which *McConnell's* holding depends?

The plurality invalidates the aggregate contribution limits for a second reason. It believes they are no longer needed to prevent contributors from circumventing federal limits on direct contributions to individuals, political parties, and political action committees. Other "campaign finance laws," combined with "experience" and "common sense," foreclose the various circumvention scenarios that the Government hypothesizes....

The plurality is wrong. Here, as in *Buckley*, in the absence of limits on aggregate political contributions, donors can and likely will find ways to channel millions of dollars to parties and to individual candidates, producing precisely the kind of "corruption" or "appearance of corruption" that previously led the Court to hold aggregate limits constitutional. Those opportunities for circumvention will also produce the type of corruption that concerns the plurality today. The methods for using today's opinion to evade the law's individual contribution limits are complex, but they are well known, or will become well known, to party fundraisers. I shall describe three.

Example One: Gifts for the Benefit of the Party. Campaign finance law permits each individual to give $64,800 over two years to a national party committee. The two major political parties each have three national committees. Federal law also entitles an individual to give $20,000 to a state party committee over two years. Each major political party has 50 such committees. Those individual limits mean that, in the absence of any aggregate limit, an individual could legally give to the Republican Party or to the Democratic Party about $1.2 million over two years. To make it easier for contributors to give gifts of this size, each party could create a "Joint Party Committee," comprising all of its national and state party committees. The titular heads could be the Speaker of the House of Representatives and the Minority Leader of the House. A contributor could then write a single check to the Joint Party Committee—and its staff would divide the funds so that each constituent unit receives no more than it could obtain from the contributor directly ($64,800 for a national committee over two years, $20,000 for a state committee over the same). Before today's decision, the total size of Rich Donor's check to the Joint Party Committee was capped at $74,600—the aggregate limit for donations to political parties over a 2-year election cycle. After today's decision, Rich Donor can write a single check to the Joint Party Committee in an amount of about $1.2 million.

Will political parties seek these large checks? Why not? The recipient national and state committees can spend the money to buy generic party advertisements, say television commercials or bumper stickers saying "Support Republicans," "Support Democrats," or the like. They also can transfer the money to party committees in battleground States to increase the chances of winning hotly contested seats....

Example Two: Donations to Individual Candidates (The $3.6 Million Check). The first example significantly understates the problem. That is because federal election law also allows a single contributor to give $5,200 to each party candidate over a 2-year election cycle (assuming the candidate is running in both a primary and a general election). There are 435 party candidates for House seats and 33 party candidates for Senate seats in any given election year. That makes an additional $2.4 million in allowable contributions. Thus, without an aggregate limit, the law will permit a wealthy individual to write a check, over a 2-year election cycle, for $3.6 million—all to benefit his political party and its candidates.

To make it easier for a wealthy donor to make a contribution of this size, the parties can simply enlarge the composition of the Joint Party Committee described in Example One, so that it now includes party candidates. And a party can proliferate such joint entities, perhaps calling the first the "Smith Victory Committee," the second the "Jones Victory Committee," and the like.

As I have just said, without any aggregate limit, the law will allow Rich Donor to write a single check to, say, the Smith Victory Committee, for up to $3.6 million. This check represents "the total amount that the contributor could contribute to all of the participants" in the Committee over a 2-year cycle. The Committee would operate under an agreement that provides a "formula for the allocation of fundraising proceeds" among its constituent units. And that "formula" would divide the proceeds so that no committee or candidate receives more than it could have received from Rich Donor directly—$64,800, $20,000, or $5,200.

So what is wrong with that? The check is considerably larger than Example One's check. But is there anything else wrong? The answer is yes, absolutely. The law will also permit a party and its candidates to shift most of Rich Donor's contributions to a single candidate, say Smith. Here is how:

The law permits each candidate and each party committee in the Smith Victory Committee to write Candidate Smith a check directly. For his primary and general elections combined, they can write checks of up to $4,000 (from each candidate's authorized campaign committee) and $10,000 (from each state and national committee). This yields a potential $1,872,000 (from candidates) plus $530,000 (from party committees). Thus, the law permits the candidates and party entities to redirect $2.37 million of Rich Donor's $3.6 million check to Candidate Smith. It also permits state and national committees to contribute to Smith's general election campaign through making coordinated expenditures—in amounts that range from $46,600 to $2.68 million for a general election (depending upon the size of Smith's State and whether he is running for a House or Senate seat).

The upshot is that Candidate Smith can receive at least $2.37 million and possibly the full $3.6 million contributed by Rich Donor to the Smith Victory Committee, even though the funds must first be divided up among the constituent units before they can be rerouted to Smith. Nothing requires the Smith Victory Committee to explain in advance to Rich Donor all of the various transfers that will take place, and nothing prevents the entities in the Committee from informing the donor and the receiving candidate after the fact what has transpired. Accordingly, the money can be donated and rerouted to Candidate Smith without the donor having violated the base limits or any other FEC regulation. . . .

Example Three: Proliferating Political Action Committees (PACs). Campaign finance law prohibits an individual from contributing (1) more than $5,200 to any candidate in a federal election cycle, and (2) more than $5,000 to a PAC in a calendar year. It also prohibits (3) any PAC from contributing more than $10,000 to any candidate in an election cycle. But the law does not prohibit an individual from contributing (within the current $123,200 biannual aggregate limit) $5,000 to each of an unlimited total number of PACs. And there, so to speak, lies the rub.

Here is how, without any aggregate limits, a party will be able to channel $2 million from each of ten Rich Donors to each of ten Embattled Candidates. Groups of party supporters—individuals, corporations, or trade unions—create

200 PACs. Each PAC claims it will use the funds it raises to support several candidates from the party, though it will favor those who are most endangered. (Each PAC qualifies for "multicandidate" status because it has received contributions from more than 50 persons and has made contributions to five federal candidates at some point previously. Over a 2-year election cycle, Rich Donor One gives $10,000 to each PAC ($5,000 per year)—yielding $2 million total. Rich Donor 2 does the same. So, too, do the other eight Rich Donors. This brings their total donations to $20 million, disbursed among the 200 PACs. Each PAC will have collected $100,000, and each can use its money to write ten checks of $10,000—to each of the ten most Embattled Candidates in the party (over two years). Every Embattled Candidate, receiving a $10,000 check from 200 PACs, will have collected $2 million.

The upshot is that ten Rich Donors will have contributed $2 million each, and ten Embattled Candidates will have collected $2 million each. In this example, unlike Example Two, the recipient candidates may not know which of the ten Rich Donors is personally responsible for the $2 million he or she receives. But the recipient candidate is highly likely to know who the ten Rich Donors are, and to feel appropriately grateful. Moreover, the ability of a small group of donors to contribute this kind of money to threatened candidates is not insignificant. In the example above—with ten Rich Donors giving $2 million each, and ten Embattled Candidates receiving $2 million each—the contributions would have been enough to finance a considerable portion of, and perhaps all of, the candidates' races in the 2012 elections.

The plurality believes that the three scenarios I have just depicted either pose no threat, or cannot or will not take place. It does not believe the scenario depicted in Example One is any cause for concern, because it involves only "general, broad-based support of a political party." Not so. A candidate who solicits a multimillion dollar check for his party will be deeply grateful to the checkwriter, and surely could reward him with a *quid pro quo* favor. The plurality discounts the scenarios depicted in Example Two and Example Three because it finds such circumvention tactics "illegal under current campaign finance laws," "implausible," or "divorced from reality." But they are not. . . .

The plurality concludes that even if circumvention were a threat, the aggregate limits are "poorly tailored" to address it. The First Amendment requires "'a fit that is . . . reasonable,'" and there is no such "fit" here because there are several alternative ways Congress could prevent evasion of the base limits. For instance, the plurality posits, Congress (or the FEC) could "tighten . . . transfer rules"; it could require "contributions above the current aggregate limits to be deposited into segregated, nontransferable accounts and spent only by their recipients"; it could define "how many candidates a PAC must support in order to ensure that 'a substantial portion' of a donor's contribution is not rerouted to a certain candidate"; or it could prohibit "donors who have contributed the current maximum sums from further contributing to political committees that have indicated they will support candidates to whom the donor has already contributed."

The plurality, however, does not show, or try to show, that these hypothetical alternatives could effectively replace aggregate contribution limits. Indeed, it does not even "opine on the validity of any particular proposal"—presumably because these proposals themselves could be subject to constitutional challenges. For the most part, the alternatives the plurality mentions were similarly available at the time of *Buckley*. Their hypothetical presence did not prevent the Court from upholding aggregate limits in 1976. How can their continued hypothetical presence lead the plurality now to conclude that aggregate limits are "poorly tailored?" How can their continued hypothetical presence lead the Court to overrule *Buckley* now?

In sum, the explanation of why aggregate limits are needed is complicated, as is the explanation of why other methods will not work. But the conclusion is simple: There is no "substantial mismatch" between Congress' legitimate objective and the "means selected to achieve it." The Court, as in *Buckley*, should hold that aggregate contribution limits are constitutional. . . .

The plurality reaches the opposite conclusion. The result, as I said at the outset, is a decision that substitutes judges' understandings of how the political process works for the understanding of Congress; that fails to recognize the difference between influence resting upon public opinion and influence bought by money alone; that overturns key precedent; that creates huge loopholes in the law; and that undermines, perhaps devastates, what remains of campaign finance reform.

With respect, I dissent.

SUPREME COURT WATCH 2014
VOLUME TWO

5

FREEDOM OF EXPRESSION AND ASSOCIATION

Writing for a unanimous Court in *Lane v. Franks*, 134 S.Ct. (2014), Justice Sotomayor reaffirmed the fifty-year-old ruling on the First Amendment free speech rights of public employees, in *Pickering v. Board of Education of Township High School District* 205, 391 U.S. 563 (1968) (discussed in Vol. 1, Ch. 8). Under the so-called *Pickering* two-part balancing test, the Court must consider "the interests of the [employee], as a citizen, in commenting upon matters of public concern" against "the interest of the State, as an employer, in promoting the efficiency of the public service through its employees." That requires, first, determining whether the employee's speech is part of his or her job; if not, then the speech is protected by the First Amendment. And, second, if the "employee spoke as a citizen on a matter of public concern," the inquiry turns to "whether the relevant governmental entity has adequate justification for treating the employee differently from any other member of the public." Here, Edward Lane, after being hired by a community college to head a youth-training program, discovered that a state representative was on the payroll but never reported for work. Lane terminated her employment and then testified in a federal prosecution for mail fraud and theft of the "representative employee," who was subsequently convicted and sentenced to thirty months in prison. Lane in turn was fired by Franks, the college president, for his actions. Applying the *Pickering* test, Justice

Sotomayor concluded that Lane's testimony was clearly protected by the First Amendment as "speech as a citizen on a matter of public concern."

B | Obscenity, Pornography, and Offensive Speech

In its 2014–2015 term the Roberts Court will consider the application of the First Amendment to social media—like Facebook and Twitter—and what constitutes a "true threat." At issue in *Elonis v. United States* (No. 13-983) is whether, consistent with the First Amendment and *Virginia v. Black* (2003) (excerpted in Vol. 2, Ch. 5), threatening another person on the Internet requires proof of subjective intent to threaten or whether it is enough to show that a "reasonable person" would regard a posted statement as threatening. Anthony Elonis is a twenty-seven-year old who was married for seven years but whose wife left him and took their two children in 2010. Shortly thereafter he was fired from his job. Subsequently, he began posting on Facebook a series of rants and rap lyrics threatening to kill his wife. On one post he talked about smothering his wife with a pillow and dumping her body in a creek. In another he wrote: "There's one way to love you but a thousand ways to kill you. I'm not going to rest until your body is a mess, soaked in blood and dying from all the little cuts. Hurry up and die, so I can bust this nut all over your corpse from atop your shallow grave. I used to be a nice guy but then you became a slut. Guess it's not your fault you liked your daddy raped you. So hurry up and die, bitch, so I can forgive you." After an FBI agent visited him, he posted similar threats and his wife got a protective order against him because, she said, "I felt like I was being stalked. I felt extremely afraid for mine and my children's and my families' lives." Elonis was tried on federal charges for threatening his wife, under a provision of the U.S. Code criminalizing the "transmitting in interstate or foreign commerce . . . any threat to injure the person of another." He was convicted and sentenced to forty-four months in prison. At trial and in his appeals, Elonis argued that he had included disclaimers in his posts, that they were "therapeutic" expressions of his depression after his wife left him and that they were more art than a threat—and thus protected by the First Amendment. On one post, for example, he wrote that "Art is about pushing limits. I'm willing to go to jail for my constitutional rights. Are you?"

H | *Symbolic Speech and Speech-Plus-Conduct*

The Court unanimously struck down Massachusetts's 2007 law establishing thirty-five-foot "buffer zones" around any abortion clinic, including public sidewalks; it was the only such statewide law, most such "buffer zones" are enacted as local ordinances in response to antiprotesters. However, in *McCullen v. Coakley*, 134 S.Ct. 2518 (2014), the Court actually split five to four with Chief Justice Roberts writing for the majority in holding that the law did not target the content or viewpoint of expression but instead was not "narrowly tailored" enough to survive First Amendment scrutiny. The Chief Justice reasoned that protesters could be arrested, without saying anything, simply because they were within a "buffer zone" and precisely for that reason the law swept too broadly. By contrast, in a concurring opinion that reads like a sharp dissent, Justice Scalia, joined by Justices Kennedy and Thomas, countered that the law did indeed target specific speech—antiabortion advocacy—and therefore was content-based discrimination that could not survive "strict scrutiny" under the First Amendment; in a separate concurring opinion, Justice Alito substantially agreed with the latter's position.

I | *Freedom of Association*

In a five-to-four ruling in *Harris v. Quinn*, 134 U.S. 2618 (2014), Justice Alito handed down a very narrow ruling that home-healthcare workers in Illinois's Medicaid program, who are non-union members and who object to paying union bargaining fees, are "partial public employees" and may not be required to contribute union dues. The Court's four most liberal justices—Justices Ginsburg, Breyer, Kagan, and Sotomayor—dissented on the ground that the decision chipped away at the power of public employee unions. But conservative groups were no less disappointed that the majority did not overrule *Abood v. Detroit Board of Education*, 431 U.S. 209 (1977), which held that the First Amendment allows the government to require public employees to pay union dues even if they are nonmembers and object to such forced association.

6

FREEDOM FROM AND OF RELIGION

A | *The (Dis)establishment of Religion*

In a major ruling on the First Amendment (dis)establishment clause, a bare majority of the Roberts Court held that prayers—predominately Christian prayers—before town council meetings do not violate the First Amendment. Writing for the Court, though only Chief Justice Roberts and Justice Alito joined the opinion, Justice Kennedy shifted the test for "the separation of church and state" from the "endorsement test" for a particular religion to the "coercion test"—whether "dissidents" who do not share the prayer's belief are "coerced" by the opening of public meetings with a prayer. In *Town of Greece, New York v. Galloway* (2014) (excerpted below), Justice Kennedy reinterpreted and extended the ruling in *Marsh v. Chambers*, 463 U.S. 783 (1983), that prayers were permissible before legislative sessions of Congress and state legislatures to local government meetings. Justice Kennedy's opinion was a kind of middle ground between that of Justices Thomas and Scalia, on the one hand, and the four dissenters, on the other. In his position for a plurality of the Court (1) prayers may be given not only at opening sessions of Congress but all state and local governmental meetings; (2) but only in the ceremonial part of the governing body's session; and (3) allow anyone in the community to deliver a prayer; (4) while also not dictating what is in the prayers, though they need not embrace the beliefs of any or multiple faiths; yet (5) such prayers may not "proselytize"—promote one faith as the true path—and criticize those of other faiths; and (6) the prayers are permissible if most of the audience is made up of adults; as well as (7) courts in reviewing challenges to governmental prayer practices should examine "the pattern of prayer" and not second-guess the content of the individual prayers given. Justice Thomas, joined by Justice Scalia, maintained that the First Amendment (dis)establishment clause did not apply to the states in the first place, and states and localities are free to include or exclude prayers from their meetings. In the major dissenting opinion, Justice Kagan, joined by Justices Ginsburg, Breyer, and Sotomayor, disputed Justice Kennedy's reinterpretation of *Marsh* and view of the underlying factual circumstances and application of the First Amendment.

Town of Greece, New York v. Galloway
134 S.Ct. 1811 (2014)

Since 1999, the monthly town board meetings in Greece, New York, opened with a roll call, a recitation of the Pledge of Allegiance, and a prayer given by clergy selected from the congregations listed in a local directory. While the prayer program is open to all creeds, nearly all of the local congregations were Christian. Susan Galloway and Linda Stephens, among others, attended meetings to speak on local issues and filed a lawsuit, alleging that the town violated the First Amendment's Establishment Clause by preferring Christians over other prayer givers and by sponsoring sectarian prayers. They sought to limit the town to "inclusive and ecumenical" prayers that referred only to a "generic God." A federal district Court upheld the prayer practice, but the U.S. Court of Appeals for the Second Circuit reversed, holding that some aspects of the prayer program, viewed in their totality by a reasonable observer, conveyed the message that the Town of Greece was endorsing Christianity. Attorneys for the Town appealed that decision and the Supreme Court granted review.

The appellate court's decision was reversed by a five-to-four vote. Justice Kennedy delivered the opinion for the Court, which only Chief Justice Roberts and Justice Alito joined. Justice Alito filed a concurring opinion, as did Justice Thomas, whose concurrence was joined by Justice Scalia. Justices Breyer and Kagan filed dissenting opinions—the latter's was joined by Justices Ginsburg, Breyer, and Sotomayor.

☐ *Justice KENNEDY delivered the opinion of the Court.*

In *Marsh v. Chambers*, 463 U.S. 783 (1983), the Court found no First Amendment violation in the Nebraska Legislature's practice of opening its sessions with a prayer delivered by a chaplain paid from state funds. The decision concluded that legislative prayer, while religious in nature, has long been understood as compatible with the Establishment Clause. As practiced by Congress since the framing of the Constitution, legislative prayer lends gravity to public business, reminds lawmakers to transcend petty differences in pursuit of a higher purpose, and expresses a common aspiration to a just and peaceful society. The Court has considered this symbolic expression to be a "tolerable acknowledgement of beliefs widely held," rather than a first, treacherous step towards establishment of a state church.

Marsh is sometimes described as "carving out an exception" to the Court's Establishment Clause jurisprudence, because it sustained legislative prayer without subjecting the practice to "any of the formal 'tests' that have traditionally structured" this inquiry. The Court in *Marsh* found those tests unnecessary because history supported the conclusion that legislative invocations are compatible with the Establishment Clause. The First Congress made it an early item of business to appoint and pay official chaplains, and both the House and Senate have maintained the office virtually uninterrupted since that time. . . .

Marsh stands for the proposition that it is not necessary to define the precise boundary of the Establishment Clause where history shows that the specific practice is permitted. Any test the Court adopts must acknowledge a practice that was accepted by the Framers and has withstood the critical scrutiny of time and political change. A test that would sweep away what has so long been settled would create new controversy and begin anew the very divisions along religious lines that the Establishment Clause seeks to prevent.

The Court's inquiry, then, must be to determine whether the prayer practice in the town of Greece fits within the tradition long followed in Congress and the state legislatures. Respondents assert that the town's prayer exercise falls outside that tradition and transgresses the Establishment Clause for two independent but mutually reinforcing reasons. First, they argue that *Marsh* did not approve prayers containing sectarian language or themes, such as the prayers offered in Greece that referred to the "death, resurrection, and ascension of the Savior Jesus Christ," and the "saving sacrifice of Jesus Christ on the cross." Second, they argue that the setting and conduct of the town board meetings create social pressures that force nonadherents to remain in the room or even feign participation in order to avoid offending the representatives who sponsor the prayer and will vote on matters citizens bring before the board. The sectarian content of the prayers compounds the subtle coercive pressures, they argue, because the nonbeliever who might tolerate ecumenical prayer is forced to do the same for prayer that might be inimical to his or her beliefs.

Respondents maintain that prayer must be nonsectarian, or not identifiable with any one religion; and they fault the town for permitting guest chaplains to deliver prayers that "use overtly Christian terms" or "invoke specifics of Christian theology." A prayer is fitting for the public sphere, in their view, only if it contains the "'most general, nonsectarian reference to God,'" and eschews mention of doctrines associated with any one faith. They argue that prayer which contemplates "the workings of the Holy Spirit, the events of Pentecost, and the belief that God 'has raised up the Lord Jesus' and 'will raise us, in our turn, and put us by His side'" would be impermissible, as would any prayer that reflects dogma particular to a single faith tradition.

An insistence on nonsectarian or ecumenical prayer as a single, fixed standard is not consistent with the tradition of legislative prayer outlined in the Court's cases. The Court found the prayers in *Marsh* consistent with the First Amendment not because they espoused only a generic theism but because our history and tradition have shown that prayer in this limited context could "coexis[t] with the principles of disestablishment and religious freedom." The Congress that drafted the First Amendment would have been accustomed to invocations containing explicitly religious themes of the sort respondents find objectionable. . . .

The contention that legislative prayer must be generic or nonsectarian derives from *dictum* in *County of Allegheny* as disputed when written and has been repudiated by later cases. There the Court held that a crèche placed on the steps of a county courthouse to celebrate the Christmas season violated the Establishment Clause because it had "the effect of endorsing a patently Christian message." Four dissenting Justices disputed that endorsement could be the proper test, as it likely would condemn a host of traditional practices that recognize the role religion plays in our society, among them legislative prayer and the "forthrightly religious" Thanksgiving proclamations issued by nearly every President since Washington. The Court sought to counter this criticism by recasting *Marsh* to permit only prayer that contained no overtly Christian references. . . .

Marsh nowhere suggested that the constitutionality of legislative prayer turns on the neutrality of its content. *Marsh* did not suggest that Nebraska's prayer practice would have failed had the chaplain not acceded to the legislator's request. Nor did the Court imply the rule that prayer violates the Establishment Clause any time it is given in the name of a figure deified by only one faith or creed. To the contrary, the Court instructed that the "content of the prayer is not of concern to judges," provided "there is no indication that the prayer opportunity has been exploited to proselytize or advance any one, or to disparage any other, faith or belief."

To hold that invocations must be nonsectarian would force the legislatures that sponsor prayers and the courts that are asked to decide these cases to act as supervisors and censors of religious speech, a rule that would involve government in religious matters to a far greater degree than is the case under the town's current practice of neither editing or approving prayers in advance nor criticizing their content after the fact. Our Government is prohibited from prescribing prayers to be recited in our public institutions in order to promote a preferred system of belief or code of moral behavior. *Engel v. Vitale*, 370 U.S. 421 (1962). . . .

In rejecting the suggestion that legislative prayer must be nonsectarian, the Court does not imply that no constraints remain on its content. The relevant constraint derives from its place at the opening of legislative sessions, where it is meant to lend gravity to the occasion and reflect values long part of the Nation's heritage. Prayer that is solemn and respectful in tone, that invites lawmakers to reflect upon shared ideals and common ends before they embark on the fractious business of governing, serves that legitimate function. If the course and practice over time shows that the invocations denigrate nonbelievers or religious minorities, threaten damnation, or preach conversion, many present may consider the prayer to fall short of the desire to elevate the purpose of the occasion and to unite lawmakers in their common effort. That circumstance would present a different case than the one presently before the Court.

The tradition reflected in *Marsh* permits chaplains to ask their own God for blessings of peace, justice, and freedom that find appreciation among people of all faiths. That a prayer is given in the name of Jesus, Allah, or Jehovah, or that it makes passing reference to religious doctrines, does not remove it from that tradition. These religious themes provide particular means to universal ends. . . .

Respondents point to other invocations that disparaged those who did not accept the town's prayer practice. One guest minister characterized objectors as a "minority" who are "ignorant of the history of our country," while another lamented that other towns did not have "God-fearing" leaders. Although these two remarks strayed from the rationale set out in *Marsh*, they do not despoil a practice that on the whole reflects and embraces our tradition. Absent a pattern of prayers that over time denigrate, proselytize, or betray an impermissible government purpose, a challenge based solely on the content of a prayer will not likely establish a constitutional violation. *Marsh*, indeed, requires an inquiry into the prayer opportunity as a whole, rather than into the contents of a single prayer.

Finally, the Court disagrees with the view taken by the Court of Appeals that the town of Greece contravened the Establishment Clause by inviting a predominantly Christian set of ministers to lead the prayer. The town made reasonable efforts to identify all of the congregations located within its borders and represented that it would welcome a prayer by any minister or layman who wished to give one. That nearly all of the congregations in town turned out to be Christian does not reflect an aversion or bias on the part of town leaders against minority faiths. . . .

Respondents further seek to distinguish the town's prayer practice from the tradition upheld in *Marsh* on the ground that it coerces participation by nonadherents. They and some *amici* contend that prayer conducted in the intimate setting of a town board meeting differs in fundamental ways from the invocations delivered in Congress and state legislatures, where the public remains segregated from legislative activity and may not address the body except by occasional invitation. Citizens attend town meetings, on the other hand, to accept awards; speak on matters of local importance; and petition the board for action that may affect their economic interests, such as the granting of permits, business licenses, and zoning variances. Respondents argue that the public may feel subtle pressure to participate in prayers that violate their beliefs in order to please the board members from whom they are about to seek a favorable ruling. In their view the fact that board members in small towns know many of their constituents by name only increases the pressure to conform.

It is an elemental First Amendment principle that government may not coerce its citizens "to support or participate in any religion or its exercise." On the record in this case the Court is not persuaded that the town of Greece, through the act of offering a brief, solemn, and respectful prayer to open its monthly meetings, compelled its citizens to engage in a religious observance. The inquiry remains a fact-sensitive one that considers both the setting in which the prayer arises and the audience to whom it is directed.

The prayer opportunity in this case must be evaluated against the backdrop of historical practice. As a practice that has long endured, legislative prayer has become part of our heritage and tradition, part of our expressive idiom, similar to the Pledge of Allegiance, inaugural prayer, or the recitation of "God save the United States and this honorable Court" at the opening of this Court's sessions. It is presumed that the reasonable observer is acquainted with this tradition and understands that its purposes are to lend gravity to public proceedings and to acknowledge the place religion holds in the lives of many private citizens, not to afford government an opportunity to proselytize or force truant constituents into the pews.

The principal audience for these invocations is not, indeed, the public but lawmakers themselves, who may find that a moment of prayer or quiet reflection sets the mind to a higher purpose and thereby eases the task of governing. . . .

The analysis would be different if town board members directed the public to participate in the prayers, singled out dissidents for opprobrium, or indicated that their decisions might be influenced by a person's acquiescence in the prayer opportunity. No such thing occurred in the town of Greece. Although board members themselves stood, bowed their heads, or made the sign of the cross during the prayer, they at no point solicited similar gestures by the public. . . .

In their declarations in the trial court, respondents stated that the prayers gave them offense and made them feel excluded and disrespected. Offense, however, does not equate to coercion. Adults often encounter speech they find disagreeable; and an Establishment Clause violation is not made out any time a person experiences a sense of affront from the expression of contrary religious views in a legislative forum, especially where, as here, any member of the public is welcome in turn to offer an invocation reflecting his or her own convictions. If circumstances arise in which the pattern and practice of ceremonial, legislative prayer is alleged to be a means to coerce or intimidate others, the objection can be addressed in the regular course. But the showing has not been made here, where the prayers neither chastised dissenters nor attempted lengthy disquisition on religious dogma. Courts remain free to review the pattern of prayers over time to determine whether they comport with the tradition of solemn, respectful prayer approved in *Marsh*, or whether coercion is a real and substantial likelihood. . . .

This case can be distinguished from the conclusions and holding of *Lee v. Weisman*. There the Court found that, in the context of a graduation where school authorities maintained close supervision over the conduct of the students and the substance of the ceremony, a religious invocation was coercive as to an objecting student. Four Justices dissented in *Lee*, but the circumstances the Court confronted there are not present in this case and do not control its outcome. Nothing in the record suggests that members of the public are dissuaded from leaving the meeting room during the prayer, arriving late, or even, as happened here, making a later protest. In this case, as in *Marsh*, board members and constituents are "free to enter and leave with little comment and for any number of reasons." . . .

In the town of Greece, the prayer is delivered during the ceremonial portion of the town's meeting. Board members are not engaged in policy-making at this time, but in more general functions, such as swearing in new police officers, inducting high school athletes into the town hall of fame, and presenting proclamations to volunteers, civic groups, and senior citizens. . . .

Ceremonial prayer is but a recognition that, since this Nation was founded and until the present day, many Americans deem that their own existence must be understood by precepts far beyond the authority of government to alter or define and that willing participation in civic affairs can be consistent with a brief acknowledgment of their belief in a higher power, always with due respect for those who adhere to other beliefs. The prayer in this case has a permissible ceremonial purpose. It is not an unconstitutional establishment of religion. . . .

☐ *Justice ALITO, with whom Justice SCALIA joins, concurring.*

I write separately to respond to the principal dissent, which really consists of two very different but intertwined opinions. One is quite narrow; the other is sweeping. I will address both. . . .

I turn now to the narrow aspect of the principal dissent, and what we find here is that the principal dissent's objection, in the end, is really quite niggling. According to the principal dissent, the town could have avoided any constitutional problem in either of two ways.

First, the principal dissent writes, "[i]f the Town Board had let its chaplains know that they should speak in nonsectarian terms, common to diverse religious groups, then no one would have valid grounds for complaint." "Priests and ministers, rabbis and imams," the principal dissent continues, "give such invocations all the time" without any great difficulty.

Both Houses of Congress now advise guest chaplains that they should keep in mind that they are addressing members from a variety of faith traditions, and as a matter of policy, this advice has much to recommend it. But any argument that nonsectarian prayer is constitutionally required runs headlong into a long history of contrary congressional practice. From the beginning, as the Court notes, many Christian prayers were offered in the House and Senate, and when rabbis and other non-Christian clergy have served as guest chaplains, their prayers have often been couched in terms particular to their faith traditions.

Not only is there no historical support for the proposition that only generic prayer is allowed, but as our country has become more diverse, composing a prayer that is acceptable to all members of the community who hold religious beliefs has become harder and harder. It was one thing to compose a prayer that is acceptable to both Christians and Jews; it is much harder to compose a prayer that is also acceptable to followers of Eastern religions that are now well represented in this country. . . .

If a town wants to avoid the problems associated with this first option, the principal dissent argues, it has another choice: It may "invit[e] clergy of many faiths." "When one month a clergy member refers to Jesus, and the next to Allah or Jehovah," the principal dissent explains, "the government does not identify itself with one religion or align itself with that faith's citizens, and the effect of even sectarian prayer is transformed."

If, as the principal dissent appears to concede, such a rotating system would obviate any constitutional problems, then despite all its high rhetoric, the principal dissent's quarrel with the town of Greece really boils down to this: The town's clerical employees did a bad job in compiling the list of potential guest chaplains. For that is really the only difference between what the town did and what the principal dissent is willing to accept. . . .

The informal, imprecise way in which the town lined up guest chaplains is typical of the way in which many things are done in small and medium-sized units of local government. In such places, the members of the governing body almost always have day jobs that occupy much of their time. The town almost never has a legal office and instead relies for legal advice on a local attorney whose practice is likely to center on such things as land-use regulation, contracts, and torts. When a municipality like the town of Greece seeks in good faith to emulate the congressional practice on which our holding in *Marsh v. Chambers* was largely based, that municipality should not be held to have violated the Constitution simply because its method of recruiting guest chaplains lacks the demographic exactitude that might be regarded as optimal. . . .

While the principal dissent, in the end, would demand no more than a small modification in the procedure that the town of Greece initially followed, much of the rhetoric in that opinion sweeps more broadly. Indeed, the logical thrust of many of its arguments is that prayer is never permissible prior to meetings of local government legislative bodies. At Greece Town Board meetings, the principal dissent pointedly notes, ordinary citizens (and even children!) are often present. The guest chaplains stand in front of the room facing the public. "[T]he setting is intimate," and ordinary citizens are permitted to speak and to ask the board to address problems that have a direct effect on their lives. The meetings are "occasions for ordinary citizens to engage with and petition their government, often on highly individualized matters." Before a session of this sort, the principal dissent argues, any prayer that is not acceptable to all in attendance is out of bounds.

The features of Greece meetings that the principal dissent highlights are by no means unusual. It is common for residents to attend such meetings, either to speak on matters on the agenda or to request that the town address other issues that are important to them. Nor is there anything unusual about the occasional attendance of students, and when a prayer is given at the beginning of such a meeting, I expect that the chaplain generally stands at the front of the room and faces the public. To do otherwise would probably be seen by many as rude. Finally, although the principal dissent attaches importance to the fact that guest chaplains in the town of Greece often began with the words "Let us pray," that is also commonplace and for many clergy, I suspect, almost reflexive. In short, I see nothing out of the ordinary about any of the features that the principal dissent notes. . . .

There can be little doubt that the decision in *Marsh* reflected the original understanding of the First Amendment. It is virtually inconceivable that the First Congress, having appointed chaplains whose responsibilities prominently included the delivery of prayers at the beginning of each daily session, thought that this practice was inconsistent with the Establishment Clause. And since this practice was well established and undoubtedly well known, it seems equally clear that the state legislatures that ratified the First Amendment had the same understanding. In the case before us, the Court of Appeals appeared to base its decision on one of the Establishment Clause "tests" set out in the opinions of this Court, but if there is any inconsistency between any of those tests and the historic practice of legislative prayer, the inconsistency calls into question the validity of the test, not the historic practice. . . .

☐ *Justice THOMAS, with whom Justice SCALIA joins, concurring.*

The Establishment Clause provides that "Congress shall make no law respecting an establishment of religion." As I have explained before, the text and history of the Clause "resis[t] incorporation" against the States. [*Elk Grove Unified School District v. Newdow*, 542 U.S. 1 (2004) (THOMAS, con. op.)]. If the Establishment Clause is not incorporated, then it has no application here, where only municipal action is at issue.

As an initial matter, the Clause probably prohibits Congress from establishing a national religion. That choice of language—"Congress shall make no law"—effectively denied Congress any power to regulate state establishments.

Construing the Establishment Clause as a federalism provision accords with the variety of church-state arrangements that existed at the Founding. At least six States had established churches in 1789. New England States like Massachusetts, Connecticut, and New Hampshire maintained local-rule establishments whereby the majority in each town could select the minister and religious denomination (usually Congregationalism, or "Puritanism"). In the South, Maryland, South Carolina, and Georgia eliminated their exclusive Anglican establishments following the American Revolution and adopted general establishments, which permitted taxation in support of all Christian churches (or, as in South Carolina, all Protestant churches). Virginia, by contrast, had recently abolished its official state establishment and ended direct government funding of clergy after a legislative battle led by James Madison. Other

States—principally Rhode Island, Pennsylvania, and Delaware, which were founded by religious dissenters—had no history of formal establishments at all, although they still maintained religious tests for office. The import of this history is that the relationship between church and state in the fledgling Republic was far from settled at the time of ratification. Although the remaining state establishments were ultimately dismantled— Massachusetts, the last State to disestablish, would do so in 1833—that outcome was far from assured when the Bill of Rights was ratified in 1791. That lack of consensus suggests that the First Amendment was simply agnostic on the subject of state establishments; the decision to establish or disestablish religion was reserved to the States.

The Federalist logic of the original Establishment Clause poses a special barrier to its mechanical incorporation against the States through the Fourteenth Amendment. Unlike the Free Exercise Clause, which "plainly protects individuals against congressional interference with the right to exercise their religion," the Establishment Clause "does not purport to protect individual rights." Instead, the States are the particular beneficiaries of the Clause. Incorporation therefore gives rise to a paradoxical result: Applying the Clause against the States eliminates their right to establish a religion free from federal interference, thereby "prohibit[ing] exactly what the Establishment Clause protected."

Put differently, the structural reasons that counsel against incorporating the Tenth Amendment also apply to the Establishment Clause. To my knowledge, no court has ever suggested that the Tenth Amendment, which "reserve[s] to the States" powers not delegated to the Federal Government, could or should be applied against the States. To incorporate that limitation would be to divest the States of all powers not specifically delegated to them, thereby inverting the original import of the Amendment. Incorporating the Establishment Clause has precisely the same effect. . . .

Even if the Establishment Clause were properly incorporated against the States, the municipal prayers at issue in this case bear no resemblance to the coercive state establishments that existed at the founding. "The coercion that was a hallmark of historical establishments of religion was coercion of religious orthodoxy and of financial support by force of law and threat of penalty." *Lee v. Weisman*, 505 U.S. 577 (1992) (SCALIA, J., dissenting). In a typical case, attendance at the established church was mandatory, and taxes were levied to generate church revenue. Dissenting ministers were barred from preaching, and political participation was limited to members of the established church. . . .

Thus, to the extent coercion is relevant to the Establishment Clause analysis, it is actual legal coercion that counts—not the "subtle coercive pressures" allegedly felt by respondents in this case. The majority properly concludes that "[o]ffense . . . does not equate to coercion," since "[a]dults often encounter speech they find disagreeable[,] and an Establishment Clause violation is not made out any time a person experiences a sense of affront from the expression of contrary religious views in a legislative forum." I would simply add, in light of the foregoing history of the Establishment Clause, that "[p]eer pressure, unpleasant as it may be, is not coercion" either.

□ *Justice BREYER, dissenting.*

As we all recognize, this is a "fact-sensitive" case. The Court of Appeals did not believe that the Constitution forbids legislative prayers that incorporate content associated with a particular denomination. Rather, the court's holding took that content into account simply because it indicated that the town had not followed a sufficiently inclusive "prayer-giver selection process." It also took into account related "actions (and inactions) of prayer-givers and town officials." Those actions and inactions included (1) a selection process that led to the selection of "clergy almost exclusively from places of worship located within the town's borders," despite the likelihood that significant numbers of town residents were members of congregations that gather just outside those borders; (2) a failure to "infor[m] members of the general public that volunteers" would be acceptable prayer givers; and (3) a failure to "infor[m] prayer-givers that invocations were not to be exploited as an effort to convert others to the particular faith of the invocational speaker, nor to disparage any faith or belief different than that of the invocational speaker."

The Court of Appeals further emphasized what it was not holding. It did not hold that "the town may not open its public meetings with a prayer," or that "any prayers offered in this context must be blandly 'nonsectarian.'" In essence, the Court of Appeals merely held that the town must do more than it had previously done to try to make its prayer practices inclusive of other faiths. And it did not prescribe a single constitutionally required method for doing so.

In my view, the Court of Appeals' conclusion and its reasoning are convincing. Justice KAGAN's dissent is consistent with that view, and I join it. . . .

☐ *Justice KAGAN, with whom Justice GINSBERG, Justice BREYER, and Justice SOTOMAYOR join, dissenting.*

For centuries now, people have come to this country from every corner of the world to share in the blessing of religious freedom. Our Constitution promises that they may worship in their own way, without fear of penalty or danger, and that in itself is a momentous offering. Yet our Constitution makes a commitment still more remarkable—that however those individuals worship, they will count as full and equal American citizens. A Christian, a Jew, a Muslim (and so forth)—each stands in the same relationship with her country, with her state and local communities, and with every level and body of government. So that when each person performs the duties or seeks the benefits of citizenship, she does so not as an adherent to one or another religion, but simply as an American.

I respectfully dissent from the Court's opinion because I think the Town of Greece's prayer practices violate that norm of religious equality—the breathtakingly generous constitutional idea that our public institutions belong no less to the Buddhist or Hindu than to the Methodist or Episcopalian. I do not contend that principle translates here into a bright separationist line. To the contrary, I agree with the Court's decision in *Marsh v. Chambers* upholding the Nebraska Legislature's tradition of beginning each session with a chaplain's prayer. And I believe that pluralism and inclusion in a town hall can satisfy the constitutional requirement of neutrality; such a forum need not become a religion-free zone. But still, the Town of Greece should lose this case. The practice at issue here differs from the one sustained in *Marsh* because Greece's town meetings involve participation by ordinary citizens, and the invocations given—directly to those citizens—were predominantly sectarian in content. Still more, Greece's Board did nothing to recognize religious diversity: In arranging for clergy members to open each meeting, the Town never sought (except briefly when this suit was filed) to involve, accommodate, or in any way reach out to adherents of non-Christian religions. So month in and month out for over a decade, prayers steeped in only one faith, addressed toward members of the public, commenced meetings to discuss local affairs and distribute government benefits. In my view, that practice does not square with the First Amendment's promise that every citizen, irrespective of her religion, owns an equal share in her government.

To begin to see what has gone wrong in the Town of Greece, consider several hypothetical scenarios in which sectarian prayer—taken straight from this case's record—infuses governmental activities. None involves, as this case does, a proceeding that could be characterized as a legislative session, but they are useful to elaborate some general principles. In each instance, assume (as was true in Greece) that the invocation is given pursuant to government policy and is representative of the prayers generally offered in the designated setting:

You are a party in a case going to trial; let's say you have filed suit against the government for violating one of your legal rights. The judge bangs his gavel to call the court to order, asks a minister to come to the front of the room, and instructs the 10 or so individuals present to rise for an opening prayer. The clergyman faces those in attendance and says: "Lord, God of all creation, ... We acknowledge the saving sacrifice of Jesus Christ on the cross. We draw strength . . . from his resurrection at Easter. Jesus Christ, who took away the sins of the world, destroyed our death, through his dying and in his rising, he has restored our life. Blessed are you, who has raised up the Lord Jesus, you who will raise us, in our turn, and put us by His side. . . . Amen." The judge then asks your lawyer to begin the trial.

It's election day, and you head over to your local polling place to vote. As you and others wait to give your names and receive your ballots, an election official asks everyone there to join him in prayer. He says: "We pray this [day] for the guidance of the Holy Spirit as [we vote]. . . . Let's just say the Our Father together. 'Our Father, who art in Heaven, hallowed be thy name; thy Kingdom come, thy will be done, on earth as it is in Heaven. . . .'" And after he concludes, he makes the sign of the cross, and appears to wait expectantly for you and the other prospective voters to do so too.

You are an immigrant attending a naturalization ceremony to finally become a citizen. The presiding official tells you and your fellow applicants that before administering the oath of allegiance, he would like a minister to pray for you and with you. The pastor steps to the front of the room, asks everyone to bow their heads, and recites: "[F]ather, son, and Holy Spirit—it is with a due sense of reverence and awe that we come before you [today] seeking your blessing. . . . You are . . . a wise God, oh Lord, . . . as evidenced even in the plan of redemption that is fulfilled in Jesus Christ. We ask that you would give freely and abundantly wisdom to one and to all . . . in the name of the Lord and Savior Jesus Christ, who lives with you and the Holy Spirit, one God for ever and ever. Amen."

I would hold that the government officials responsible for the above practices—that is, for prayer repeatedly invoking a single religion's beliefs in these settings—crossed a constitutional line. I have every confidence the Court would agree. Why?

The reason, of course, has nothing to do with Christianity as such. This opinion is full of Christian prayers, because those were the only invocations offered in the Town of Greece. But if my hypotheticals involved the prayer of some other religion, the outcome would be exactly the same. . . .

And making matters still worse: They have done so in a place where individuals come to interact with, and participate in, the institutions and processes of their government. A person goes to court, to the polls, to a naturalization ceremony—and a government official or his hand-picked minister asks her, as the first order of official business, to stand and pray with others in a way conflicting with her own religious beliefs. Perhaps she feels sufficient pressure to go along—to rise, bow her head, and join in whatever others are saying: After all, she wants, very badly, what the judge or poll worker or immigration official has to offer. Or perhaps she is made of stronger mettle, and she opts not to participate in what she does not believe—indeed, what would, for her, be something like blasphemy. She then must make known her dissent from the common religious view, and place herself apart from other citizens, as well as from the officials responsible for the invocations. And so a civic function of some kind brings religious differences to the fore: That public proceeding becomes (whether intentionally or not) an instrument for dividing her from adherents to the community's majority religion, and for altering the very nature of her relationship with her government.

That is not the country we are, because that is not what our Constitution permits. Here, when a citizen stands before her government, whether to perform a service or request a benefit, her religious beliefs do not enter into the picture. . . .

[N]o one can fairly read the prayers from Greece's Town meetings as anything other than explicitly Christian—constantly and exclusively so. From the time Greece established its prayer practice in 1999 until litigation loomed nine years later, all of its monthly chaplains were Christian clergy. And after a brief spell surrounding the filing of this suit (when a Jewish layman, a Wiccan priestess, and a Baha'i minister appeared at meetings), the Town resumed its practice of inviting only clergy from neighboring Protestant and Catholic churches. About two-thirds of the prayers given over this decade or so invoked "Jesus," "Christ," "Your Son," or "the Holy Spirit"; in the 18 months before the record closed, 85% included those references. And the prayers usually close with phrases like "in the name of Jesus Christ" or "in the name of Your son."

Still more, the prayers betray no understanding that the American community is today, as it long has been, a rich mosaic of religious faiths. The monthly chaplains appear almost always to assume that everyone in the room is Christian (and of a kind who has no objection to government-sponsored worship). . . .

To recap: *Marsh* upheld prayer addressed to legislators alone, in a proceeding in which citizens had no role—and even then, only when it did not "proselytize or advance" any single religion. It was that legislative prayer practice (not every prayer in a body exercising any legislative function) that the Court found constitutional given its "unambiguous and unbroken history." But that approved practice, as I have shown, is not Greece's. None of the history *Marsh* cited—and none the majority details today—supports calling on citizens to pray, in a manner consonant with only a single religion's beliefs, at a participatory public proceeding, having both legislative and adjudicative components. Or to use the majority's phrase, no "history shows that th[is] specific practice is permitted." And so, contra the majority, Greece's prayers cannot simply ride on the constitutional coattails of the legislative tradition *Marsh* described. . . .

None of this means that Greece's town hall must be religion- or prayer-free. "[W]e are a religious people," *Marsh* observed, and prayer draws some warrant from tradition in a town hall, as well as in Congress or a state legislature. What the circumstances here demand is the recognition that we are a pluralistic people too. When citizens of all faiths come to speak to each other and their elected representatives in a legislative session, the government must take especial care to ensure that the prayers they hear will seek to include, rather than serve to divide. No more is required—but that much is crucial—to treat every citizen, of whatever religion, as an equal participant in her government. And contrary to the majority's (and Justice ALITO's) view, that is not difficult to do. If the Town Board had let its chaplains know that they should speak in nonsectarian terms, common to diverse religious groups, then no one would have valid grounds for complaint. Priests and ministers, rabbis and imams give such invocations all the time; there is no great mystery to the project. Or if the Board preferred, it might have invited clergy of many faiths to serve as chaplains, as the majority notes that Congress does. When one month a clergy member refers to Jesus, and the next to Allah or Jehovah—as the majority hopefully though counterfactually suggests happened here— the government does not identify itself with one religion or align itself with that faith's citizens, and the effect of even sectarian prayer is transformed. So Greece had multiple ways of incorporating prayer into its town meetings— reflecting all the ways that prayer (as most of us know from daily life) can forge common bonds, rather than divide.

But Greece could not do what it did: infuse a participatory government body with one (and only one) faith, so that month in and month out, the citizens appearing before it become partly defined by their creed—as those who share, and those who do not, the community's majority religious belief. In this country, when citizens go before the government, they go not as Christians or Muslims or Jews (or what have you), but just as Americans (or here, as Grecians). That is what it means to be an equal citizen, irrespective of religion. And that is what the Town of Greece precluded by so identifying itself with a single faith.

How, then, does the majority go so far astray, allowing the Town of Greece to turn its assemblies for citizens into a forum for Christian prayer? The answer does not lie in first principles: I have no doubt that every member of this Court believes as firmly as I that our institutions of government belong equally to all, regardless of faith. Rather, the error reflects two kinds of blindness. First, the majority misapprehends the facts of this case, as distinct from those characterizing traditional legislative prayer. And second, the majority misjudges the essential meaning of the religious worship in Greece's town hall, along with its capacity to exclude and divide.

The facts here matter to the constitutional issue; indeed, the majority itself acknowledges that the requisite inquiry—a "fact-sensitive" one—turns on "the setting in which the prayer arises and the audience to whom it is directed." But then the majority glides right over those considerations—at least as they relate to the Town of Greece. When the majority analyzes the "setting" and "audience" for prayer, it focuses almost exclusively on Congress and the Nebraska Legislature, it does not stop to analyze how far those factors differ in Greece's meetings. The majority thus gives short shrift to the gap—more like, the chasm—between a legislative floor session involving only elected officials and a town hall revolving around ordinary citizens. And similarly the majority neglects to consider how the prayers in Greece are mostly addressed to members of the public, rather than (as in the forums it discusses) to the lawmakers. "The District Court in *Marsh*," the majority expounds, "described the prayer exercise as 'an internal act' directed at the Nebraska Legislature's 'own members.'" Well, yes, so it is in Lincoln, and on Capitol Hill. But not in Greece, where as I have described, the chaplain faces the Town's residents—with the Board watching from on high—and calls on them to pray together.

And of course—as the majority sidesteps as well—to pray in the name of Jesus Christ. In addressing the sectarian content of these prayers, the majority again changes the subject, preferring to explain what happens in other government bodies. The majority notes, for example, that Congress "welcom[es] ministers of many creeds," who commonly speak of "values that count as universal," and in that context, the majority opines, the fact "[t]hat a prayer is given in the name of Jesus, Allah, or Jehovah . . . does not remove it from" *Marsh's* protection. But that case is not this one, as I have shown, because in Greece only Christian clergy members speak, and then mostly in the voice of their own religion; no Allah or Jehovah ever is mentioned. So all the majority can point to in the Town's practice is that the Board "maintains a policy of nondiscrimination," and "represent[s] that it would welcome a prayer by any minister or layman who wishe[s] to give one." But that representation has never been publicized; nor has the Board (except for a few months surrounding this suit's filing) offered the chaplain's role to any non-Christian clergy or layman, in either Greece or its environs; nor has the Board ever provided its chaplains with guidance about reaching out to members of other faiths, as most state legislatures and Congress do. The majority thus errs in assimilating the Board's prayer practice to that of Congress or the Nebraska Legislature. Unlike those models, the Board is determinedly—and relentlessly—noninclusive.

And the month in, month out sectarianism the Board chose for its meetings belies the majority's refrain that the prayers in Greece were "ceremonial" in nature. Ceremonial references to the divine surely abound: The majority is right that "the Pledge of Allegiance, inaugural prayer, or the recitation of 'God save the United States and this honorable Court' " each fits the bill. But prayers evoking "the saving sacrifice of Jesus Christ on the cross," "the plan of redemption that is fulfilled in Jesus Christ," "the life and death, resurrection and ascension of the Savior Jesus Christ," the workings of the Holy Spirit, the events of Pentecost, and the belief that God "has raised up the Lord Jesus" and "will raise us, in our turn, and put us by His side"? No. These are statements of profound belief and deep meaning, subscribed to by many, denied by some.

The content of Greece's prayers is a big deal, to Christians and non-Christians alike. A person's response to the doctrine, language, and imagery contained in those invocations reveals a core aspect of identity—who that person is and how she faces the world. And the responses of different individuals, in Greece and across this country, of course vary. Contrary to the majority's apparent view, such sectarian prayers are not "part of our expressive idiom" or "part of our heritage and tradition," assuming the word "our" refers to all Americans. They express beliefs that are fundamental to some, foreign to others—and because that is so they carry the ever-present potential to both exclude and divide. The majority, I think, assesses too lightly the significance of these religious differences, and so fears too little the "religiously based divisiveness that the Establishment Clause seeks to avoid." I would treat more seriously the multiplicity of Americans' religious commitments, along with the challenge they can pose to the project—the distinctively American project—of creating one from the many, and governing all as united. . . .

When the citizens of this country approach their government, they do so only as Americans, not as members of one faith or another. And that means that even in a partly legislative body, they should not confront government-sponsored worship that divides them along religious lines. I believe, for all the reasons I have given, that the Town of Greece betrayed that promise. . . .

B | *Free Exercise of Religion*

After a bare majority of the Roberts Court upheld, in *National Federation of Independent Business v. Sebelius*, 132 S.Ct. 2566 (2012) (excerpted in Vol. 1, Ch. 6), the main provisions of President Obama's signature piece of legislation—the Patient Protection and Affordable Care Act (ACA) of 2010 (otherwise known as "Obamacare")—conservatives, Catholics, and Evangelical Christians maintained their opposition, specifically to its requirement that healthcare programs include coverage for contraception and abortion. As a result, when implementing the law the Obama administration exempted religious groups and businesses from the contraceptive coverage provisions. Still, conservatives and some Evangelical Christians continued to oppose the law's requirement that employers provide health-insurance coverage for contraception—such as an IUD and morning-after pills—and they contend there is no difference between certain kinds of contraception and abortion. In particular, the Becket Fund for Religious Liberty spearheaded a challenge to the law based on the Religious Freedom Restoration Act (RFRA) (discussed, along with relevant excerpted cases, in Vol. 2, Ch. 6). The Evangelical owners of Hobby Lobby Stores, a multimillion-dollar for-profit corporation with over 17,000 employees in some 600 arts and crafts stores, joined forces in challenging the law because of their religious objections. At issue was whether a for-profit corporation may be exempted from the ACA's requirements for contraceptive coverage because of the guarantees for religious freedom under the RFRA. Federal appellate courts were split on the controversy. The Court of Appeals for the Tenth Circuit ruled that forcing Hobby Lobby to pay for contraceptive coverage violated the RFRA. But the appellate court for the third circuit ruled otherwise in another suit, over a Pennsylvania-based Mennonite cabinet-making company's refusal to comply with the mandated contraceptive coverage. Hence the Supreme Court granted review and consolidated the cases.

In a bitter five-to-four decision in *Burwell v. Hobby Lobby Stores, Inc.*, 134 U.S. 2751 (2014), Justice Alito held that the RFRA's religious freedom exemptions apply to "closely held for-profit corporations," like Hobby Lobby Stores, and they are exempt from providing employees with contraceptive coverage under the ACA. Justice Alito underscored in a forty-nine-page opinion that the ruling did not apply to large corporations not controlled by a family or small group with religious objections to contraceptives and abortion. Nor did the ruling, Justice Alito emphasized, apply to healthcare coverage for blood transfusions, vaccinations, or other medical procedures objected to on religious grounds. In a four-page concurring opinion, Justice Kennedy responded to the four dissenters in cautioning that the decision "does not have the breadth and sweep ascribed to it by the respectful and powerful dissent." But Justice Ginsburg's thirty-five-page dissent—joined by Justices Breyer, Sotomayor, and Kagan—contended that the Court's bare-majority had indeed rendered a "decision of startling breadth" in (1) acknowledging that corporations, like individuals, may claim religious exemption from regulations and (2) permitting employers to deny women certain healthcare benefits because of a "closely held corporation's" religious objections. Although the ruling in *Hobby Lobby Stores* was only a statutory (not a constitutional) decision, it is certain to invite further litigation over the religious objections of individuals and corporations to complying with laws barring discrimination against women, gay and lesbian couples, and others.

7

THE FOURTH AMENDMENT GUARANTEE AGAINST UNREASONABLE SEARCHES AND SEIZURES

In a major ruling on the application of the Fourth Amendment in the twenty-first-century digital age, the Roberts Court unanimously held in *Riley v. California* (2014) (excerpted below) that police must generally obtain a search warrant for searching cell phones even after arresting a person and taking them into custody.

Riley v. California
134 S.Ct. 2473 (2014)

In a major ruling on the application of the Fourth Amendment in the digital age, the Roberts Court held that police must generally obtain a search warrant in order to search the cell phone of a person who has been arrested.

David Riley was stopped for a traffic violation and arrested on weapons charges. An officer searching Riley incident to the arrest seized a cell phone from Riley's pants pocket. The officer accessed information on the phone and noticed the repeated use of a term associated with a street gang. At the police station two hours later, a detective specializing in gangs further examined the phone's digital contents. Based in part on photographs and videos that the detective found, Riley was charged with a gang-related shooting. Riley's attorney moved to suppress all evidence that the police had obtained from his cell phone. The trial court denied the motion, Riley was convicted, and that decision was affirmed by a California state appellate court.

Brima Wurie was arrested after police observed him making a drug sale. At the police station, the officers seized a cell phone from Wurie's person and noticed that the phone was receiving multiple calls from a source identified as "my house." The officers opened the phone, accessed its call log, determined the number associated with the "my house" label, and traced that number to what they suspected was Wurie's apartment. They secured a search warrant and found drugs, a firearm and ammunition, and cash. Wurie was then charged with drug and firearm offenses. He moved to suppress the evidence obtained from the search of the apartment. A federal district court denied the motion, Wurie was convicted, and a federal appellate court reversed the denial of the motion to suppress and vacated Wurie's convictions.

On appeal, the Supreme Court reversed the state court's decision in Riley's case and affirmed the federal appellate court's decision in Wurie's case. Chief Justice Roberts delivered the opinion of a unanimous Court. Justice Alito filed a concurring opinion.

☐ *CHIEF JUSTICE ROBERTS delivered the opinion of the Court.*

The Fourth Amendment provides: "The right of the people to be secure in their persons, houses, papers, and effects, against unreasonable searches and seizures, shall not be violated, and no Warrants shall issue, but upon probable cause, supported by Oath or affirmation, and particularly describing the place to be searched, and the persons or things to be seized."

As the text makes clear, "the ultimate touchstone of the Fourth Amendment is 'reasonableness.'" Our cases have determined that "[w]here a search is undertaken by law enforcement officials to discover evidence of criminal wrongdoing . . . reasonableness generally requires the obtaining of a judicial warrant." *Vernonia School Dist. 47J v. Acton*, 515 U.S. 646 (1995). Such a warrant ensures that the inferences to support a search are "drawn by a neutral and detached magistrate instead of being judged by the officer engaged in the often competitive enterprise of ferreting out crime." *Johnson v. United States*, 333 U.S. 10 (1948). In the absence of a warrant, a search is reasonable only if it falls within a specific exception to the warrant requirement.

The two cases before us concern the reasonableness of a warrantless search incident to a lawful arrest. In 1914, this Court first acknowledged in dictum "the right on the part of the Government, always recognized under English and American law, to search the person of the accused when legally arrested to discover and seize the fruits or evidences of crime." *Weeks v. United States*, 232 U.S. 383. Since that time, it has been well accepted that such a search constitutes an exception to the warrant requirement. Indeed, the label "exception" is something of a misnomer in this context, as warrantless searches incident to arrest occur with far greater frequency than searches conducted pursuant to a warrant.

Although the existence of the exception for such searches has been recognized for a century, its scope has been debated for nearly as long. See *Arizona v. Gant*, 556 U.S. 332 (2009). That debate has focused on the extent to which officers may search property found on or near the arrestee. Three related precedents set forth the rules governing such searches:

The first, *Chimel v. California*, 395 U.S. 752 (1969), laid the groundwork for most of the existing search incident to arrest doctrine. Police officers in that case arrested Chimel inside his home and proceeded to search his entire three-bedroom house, including the attic and garage. In particular rooms, they also looked through the contents of drawers.

The Court crafted the following rule for assessing the reasonableness of a search incident to arrest: "When an arrest is made, it is reasonable for the arresting officer to search the person arrested in order to remove any weapons that the latter might seek to use in order to resist arrest or effect his escape. Otherwise, the officer's safety might well be endangered, and the arrest itself frustrated. In addition, it is entirely reasonable for the arresting officer to search for and seize any evidence on the arrestee's person in order to prevent its concealment or destruction. . . . There is ample justification, therefore, for a search of the arrestee's person and the area 'within his immediate control'—construing that phrase to mean the area from within which he might gain possession of a weapon or destructible evidence."

The extensive warrantless search of Chimel's home did not fit within this exception, because it was not needed to protect officer safety or to preserve evidence. Four years later, in *United States v. Robinson*, 414 U.S. 218 (1973), the Court applied the *Chimel* analysis in the context of a search of the arrestee's person. A police officer had arrested Robinson for driving with a revoked license. The officer conducted a patdown search and felt an object that he could not identify in Robinson's coat pocket. He removed the object, which turned out to be a crumpled cigarette package, and opened it. Inside were 14 capsules of heroin.

[T]he search of Robinson was reasonable even though there was no concern about the loss of evidence, and the arresting officer had no specific concern that Robinson might be armed. In doing so, the Court did not draw a line between a search of Robinson's person and a further examination of the cigarette pack found during that search. It merely noted that, "[h]aving in the course of a lawful search come upon the crumpled package of cigarettes, [the officer] was entitled to inspect it." A few years later, the Court clarified that this exception was limited to "personal property . . . immediately associated with the person of the arrestee." *United States v. Chadwick*, 433 U.S. 1 (1977) (200-pound, locked footlocker could not be searched incident to arrest), abrogated on other grounds by *California v. Acevedo*, 500 U.S. 565 (1991).

The search incident to arrest trilogy concludes with *Gant*, which analyzed searches of an arrestee's vehicle. *Gant*, like *Robinson*, recognized that the *Chimel* concerns for officer safety and evidence preservation underlie the search incident to arrest exception. As a result, the Court concluded that *Chimel* could authorize police to search a vehicle "only when the arrestee is unsecured and within reaching distance of the passenger compartment at the time of the search." *Gant* added, however, an independent exception for a warrantless search of a vehicle's passenger compartment "when it is 'reasonable to believe evidence relevant to the crime of arrest might be found in the vehicle.'" That exception stems not from *Chimel*, the Court explained, but from "circumstances unique to the vehicle context."

These cases require us to decide how the search incident to arrest doctrine applies to modern cell phones, which are now such a pervasive and insistent part of daily life that the proverbial visitor from Mars might conclude they were an important feature of human anatomy. A smart phone of the sort taken from Riley was unheard of ten years ago; a significant majority of American adults now own such phones. Even less sophisticated phones like Wurie's, which have already faded in popularity since Wurie was arrested in 2007, have been around for less than 15 years. Both phones are based on technology nearly inconceivable just a few decades ago, when *Chimel* and *Robinson* were decided.

Absent more precise guidance from the founding era, we generally determine whether to exempt a given type of search from the warrant requirement "by assessing, on the one hand, the degree to which it intrudes upon an individual's privacy and, on the other, the degree to which it is needed for the promotion of legitimate governmental interests." Such a balancing of interests supported the search incident to arrest exception in *Robinson*, and a mechanical application of *Robinson* might well support the warrantless searches at issue here.

But while *Robinson*'s categorical rule strikes the appropriate balance in the context of physical objects, neither of its rationales has much force with respect to digital content on cell phones. On the government interest side, *Robinson* concluded that the two risks identified in *Chimel*—harm to officers and destruction of evidence—are present in all custodial arrests. There are no comparable risks when the search is of digital data. In addition, *Robinson* regarded any privacy interests retained by an individual after arrest as significantly diminished by the fact of the arrest itself. Cell phones, however, place vast quantities of personal information literally in the hands of individuals. A search of the information on a cell phone bears little resemblance to the type of brief physical search considered in *Robinson*.

We therefore decline to extend *Robinson* to searches of data on cell phones, and hold instead that officers must generally secure a warrant before conducting such a search. . . .

Digital data stored on a cell phone cannot itself be used as a weapon to harm an arresting officer or to effectuate the arrestee's escape. Law enforcement officers remain free to examine the physical aspects of a phone to ensure that it will not be used as a weapon—say, to determine whether there is a razor blade hidden between the phone and its case. Once an officer has secured a phone and eliminated any potential physical threats, however, data on the phone can endanger no one.

Perhaps the same might have been said of the cigarette pack seized from Robinson's pocket. Once an officer gained control of the pack, it was unlikely that Robinson could have accessed the pack's contents. But unknown physical objects may always pose risks, no matter how slight, during the tense atmosphere of a custodial arrest. The officer in *Robinson* testified that he could not identify the objects in the cigarette pack but knew they were not cigarettes. Given that, a further search was a reasonable protective measure. No such unknowns exist with respect to digital data. . . .

The United States and California focus primarily on the second *Chimel* rationale: preventing the destruction of evidence.

Both Riley and Wurie concede that officers could have seized and secured their cell phones to prevent destruction of evidence while seeking a warrant.

That is a sensible concession. And once law enforcement officers have secured a cell phone, there is no longer any risk that the arrestee himself will be able to delete incriminating data from the phone.

The United States and California argue that information on a cell phone may nevertheless be vulnerable to two types of evidence destruction unique to digital data—remote wiping and data encryption. . . . As an initial matter, these broader concerns about the loss of evidence are distinct from *Chimel's* focus on a defendant who responds to arrest by trying to conceal or destroy evidence within his reach. With respect to remote wiping, the Government's primary concern turns on the actions of third parties who are not present at the scene of arrest. And data encryption is even further afield. There, the Government focuses on the ordinary operation of a phone's security features, apart from *any* active attempt by a defendant or his associates to conceal or destroy evidence upon arrest. . . .

In any event, as to remote wiping, law enforcement is not without specific means to address the threat. Remote wiping can be fully prevented by disconnecting a phone from the network. There are at least two simple ways to do this: First, law enforcement officers can turn the phone off or remove its battery. Second, if they are concerned about encryption or other potential problems, they can leave a phone powered on and place it in an enclosure that isolates the phone from radio waves. Such devices are commonly called "Faraday bags," after the English scientist Michael Faraday. They are essentially sandwich bags made of aluminum foil: cheap, lightweight, and easy to use. They may not be a complete answer to the problem, but at least for now they provide a reasonable response. In fact, a number of law enforcement agencies around the country already encourage the use of Faraday bags.

To the extent that law enforcement still has specific concerns about the potential loss of evidence in a particular case, there remain more targeted ways to address those concerns. If "the police are truly confronted with a 'now or never' situation,"—for example, circumstances suggesting that a defendant's phone will be the target of an imminent remote-wipe attempt—they may be able to rely on exigent circumstances to search the phone immediately.

The search incident to arrest exception rests not only on the heightened government interests at stake in a volatile arrest situation, but also on an arrestee's reduced privacy interests upon being taken into police custody. *Robinson* focused primarily on the first of those rationales. The fact that an arrestee has diminished privacy interests does not mean that the Fourth Amendment falls out of the picture entirely. Not every search "is acceptable solely because a person is in custody." To the contrary, when "privacy-related concerns are weighty enough" a "search may require a warrant, notwithstanding the diminished expectations of privacy of the arrestee." *Ibid.* One such example, of course, is *Chimel*. *Chimel* refused to "characteriz[e] the invasion of privacy that results from a top-to-bottom search of a man's house as 'minor.'" Because a search of the arrestee's entire house was a substantial invasion beyond the arrest itself, the Court concluded that a warrant was required.

Robinson is the only decision from this Court applying *Chimel* to a search of the contents of an item found on an arrestee's person. The United States asserts that a search of all data stored on a cell phone is "materially indistinguishable" from searches of these sorts of physical items. That is like saying a ride on horseback is materially indistinguishable from a flight to the moon. . . .

Cell phones differ in both a quantitative and a qualitative sense from other objects that might be kept on an arrestee's person. The term "cell phone" is itself misleading shorthand; many of these devices are in fact minicomputers that also happen to have the capacity to be used as a telephone. They could just as easily be called cameras, video players, rolodexes, calendars, tape recorders, libraries, diaries, albums, televisions, maps, or newspapers.

One of the most notable distinguishing features of modern cell phones is their immense storage capacity. Before cell phones, a search of a person was limited by physical realities and tended as a general matter to constitute only a narrow intrusion on privacy. Most people cannot lug around every piece of mail they have received for the past several months, every picture they have taken, or every book or article they have read—nor would they have any reason to attempt to do so. And if they did, they would have to drag behind them a trunk of the sort held to require a search warrant in *Chadwick*, rather than a container the size of the cigarette package in *Robinson*.

But the possible intrusion on privacy is not physically limited in the same way when it comes to cell phones. The current top-selling smart phone has a standard capacity of 16 gigabytes (and is available with up to 64 gigabytes). Sixteen gigabytes translates to millions of pages of text, thousands of pictures, or hundreds of videos. Cell phones couple that capacity with the ability to store many different types of information: Even the most basic phones that sell for less than $20 might hold photographs, picture messages, text messages, Internet browsing history, a calendar, a thousand-entry phone book, and so on. We expect that the gulf between physical practicability and digital capacity will only continue to widen in the future.

The storage capacity of cell phones has several interrelated consequences for privacy. First, a cell phone collects in one place many distinct types of information—an address, a note, a prescription, a bank statement, a video— that reveal much more in combination than any isolated record. Second, a cell phone's capacity allows even just one type of information to convey far more than previously possible. The sum of an individual's private life can be reconstructed through a thousand photographs labeled with dates, locations, and descriptions; the same cannot be said of a photograph or two of loved ones tucked into a wallet. Third, the data on a phone can date back to the purchase of the phone, or even earlier. A person might carry in his pocket a slip of paper reminding him to call Mr. Jones; he would not carry a record of all his communications with Mr. Jones for the past several months, as would routinely be kept on a phone.

Finally, there is an element of pervasiveness that characterizes cell phones but not physical records. Prior to the digital age, people did not typically carry a cache of sensitive personal information with them as they went about their day. Now it is the person who is not carrying a cell phone, with all that it contains, who is the exception. According to one poll, nearly three-quarters of smart phone users report being within five feet of their phones most of the time, with 12% admitting that they even use their phones in the shower. A decade ago police officers searching an arrestee might have occasionally stumbled across a highly personal item such as a diary. But those discoveries were likely to be few and far between. Today, by contrast, it is no exaggeration to say that many of the more than 90% of American adults who own a cell phone keep on their person a digital record of nearly every aspect of their lives—from the mundane to the intimate. Allowing the police to scrutinize such records on a routine basis is quite different from allowing them to search a personal item or two in the occasional case.

Although the data stored on a cell phone is distinguished from physical records by quantity alone, certain types of data are also qualitatively different. An Internet search and browsing history, for example, can be found on an

Internet-enabled phone and could reveal an individual's private interests or concerns—perhaps a search for certain symptoms of disease, coupled with frequent visits to WebMD. Data on a cell phone can also reveal where a person has been. Historic location information is a standard feature on many smart phones and can reconstruct someone's specific movements down to the minute, not only around town but also within a particular building.…

We cannot deny that our decision today will have an impact on the ability of law enforcement to combat crime. Cell phones have become important tools in facilitating coordination and communication among members of criminal enterprises, and can provide valuable incriminating information about dangerous criminals. Privacy comes at a cost.

Our holding, of course, is not that the information on a cell phone is immune from search; it is instead that a warrant is generally required before such a search, even when a cell phone is seized incident to arrest. Our cases have historically recognized that the warrant requirement is "an important working part of our machinery of government," not merely "an inconvenience to be somehow 'weighed' against the claims of police efficiency." *Coolidge v. New Hampshire*, 493 U.S. 443 (1971). Recent technological advances similar to those discussed here have, in addition, made the process of obtaining a warrant itself more efficient.

Moreover, even though the search incident to arrest exception does not apply to cell phones, other case-specific exceptions may still justify a warrantless search of a particular phone. "One well-recognized exception applies when 'the exigencies of the situation' make the needs of law enforcement so compelling that [a] warrantless search is objectively reasonable under the Fourth Amendment."… In light of the availability of the exigent circumstances exception, there is no reason to believe that law enforcement officers will not be able to address some of the more extreme hypotheticals that have been suggested: a suspect texting an accomplice who, it is feared, is preparing to detonate a bomb, or a child abductor who may have information about the child's location on his cell phone. The defendants here recognize—indeed, they stress—that such fact-specific threats may justify a warrantless search of cell phone data. The critical point is that, unlike the search incident to arrest exception, the exigent circumstances exception requires a court to examine whether an emergency justified a warrantless search in each particular case.…

C | The Special Problems of Automobiles in a Mobile Society

A bare majority of the Roberts Court, in an unusual voting alignment, broadened police powers to stop drivers of cars based on anonymous tips from otherwise uncorroborated 911 phone calls in holding that a 911 phone call is enough to establish a "reasonable suspicion" for police to make an investigatory stop. The ruling in *Navarette v. California*, 134 S.Ct. 1683 (2014), not only continued the trend in recent decades of decoupling the Fourth Amendments "reasonableness clause" from the "warrants clause" requirements of a search and seizure but broadened the automobile exception. The decision broadly expanded police discretion to make warrantless stops and searches based on "the totality of circumstances" standard for whether they have a "reasonable suspicion" of criminal activities, even though the 911 tip is uncorroborated. Writing for the Court, Justice Thomas held that police may make such stops based on the following reasoning and construction of the facts: First, the tipster made a 911 call about the careless and erratic driving of a truck and reported its license number. Second, the fact the tip came from a 911 call added to its reliability because such new technology allows police to identify the caller and thus go after them for making false reports. Third, the fact that a tipster described a near accident was enough for police to conclude that the driver might be drunk. Fourth, the suspicion of drunken driving, along with its hazards to the public, justified the stop, even though police did not witness any erratic driving while following the vehicle because that fact did not prove that the driver was drunk. Fifth, the suspicion of drunk driving was enough, under the Fourth Amendment, for police to stop the vehicle. And, finally, after stopping to question the driver the officers smelled marijuana and that justified a search of the truck, in which bags of marijuana were found and for which the driver and passengers were arrested and prosecuted. Chief Justice Roberts and Justices Kennedy, Breyer, and Alito joined Justice Thomas's opinion.

In a sharp dissent in *Navarette* Justice Scalia, joined by Justices Ginsburg, Sotomayor, and Kagan, took strong exception to Justice Thomas's construction of the facts and sequence of events, as well as the ultimate conclusion. In Justice Scalia's words:

> The Court's opinion serves up a freedom-destroying cocktail consisting of two parts patent falsity: (1) that anonymous 911 reports of traffic violations are reliable so long as they correctly identify a car and its location, and (2) that a single instance of careless or reckless driving necessarily supports a reasonable suspicion of drunkenness. All the malevolent 911 caller need do is assert a traffic violation, and the targeted car will be stopped, forcibly if necessary, by the police. If the driver turns out not to be drunk (which will almost always be the case), the caller need fear no consequences, even if 911 knows his identity. After all, he never alleged drunkenness, but merely called in a traffic violation—and on that point his word is as good as his victim's.
>
> Drunken driving is a serious matter, but so is the loss of our freedom to come and go as we please without police interference. To prevent and detect murder we do not allow searches without probable cause or targeted Terry stops without reasonable suspicion. We should not do so for drunken driving either. After today's opinion all of us on the road, and not just drug

dealers, are at risk of having our freedom of movement curtailed on suspicion of drunkenness, based upon a phone tip, true or false, of a single instance of careless driving.

In its 2014 term the Court will consider another case involving the basis for automobile traffic stops. *Heien v. North Carolina* (No. 13-604) raises the question of whether an officer's mistaken understanding of a statute may nonetheless create a "reasonable suspicion" justifying a traffic stop. Heien's car was pulled over for having only one brake light on, in violation of a state law requiring two brake lights. The officer issued a warning citation but then asked to search the car. Heien consented and, after a search that discovered cocaine, was arrested for drug trafficking. His attorney moved to exclude the evidence on the ground that the stop violated the Fourth Amendment because the officer lacked a "reasonable articulable suspicion that criminal activity had been committed, or that a motor vehicle traffic offense or infraction had occurred."

II

The Right of Privacy

A | *Privacy and Reproductive Freedom*

In a widely watched case a bare majority of the Roberts Court held that religious objections of a business or a "closely held corporation" to complying with the Affordable Care Act's mandatory healthcare coverage for contraceptives override the claims and interests of female employees in obtaining those benefits. All five Republican-appointed justices composed the majority, with the four Democratic-appointed justices dissenting in *Burwell v. Hobby Lobby Stores, Inc.* (2014), which is further discussed here in Chapter 6.

12

THE EQUAL PROTECTION
OF THE LAW

C | *Affirmative Action and Reverse Discrimination*

A solid majority of the Roberts Court, in *Schuette v. Coalition to Defend Affirmative Action, Integration and Immigrant Rights and Fight for Equality by Any Means Necessary (BAMN)* (2014) (excerpted below), signaled the end to court-approved affirmative-action programs in higher education and, more generally, government. Writing for the Court in a plurality opinion, joined only by Chief Justice Roberts and Justice Alito, Justice Kennedy emphasized that "This case is not about how the debate about racial preferences should be resolved. It is about who may resolve it. There is no authority in the Constitution of the United States or in this court's precedents for the judiciary to set aside Michigan laws that commit this policy determination to the voters." In other words, the issue of affirmative-action programs is in the hands of voters—at the state and local levels—and no longer for reviewing courts. That is to say, states are free to ban (as Michigan and seven other states do) or adopt affirmative-action programs. In separate concurring opinions, Chief Justice Roberts and Justice Scalia, joined by Justice Thomas, would have gone further and overturned precedents upholding affirmative action, while allowing preferences for athletes, children of alumni, and other considerations, such as wealth or applications from various geographical areas. Dissenting Justice Sotomayor, joined by Justice Ginsburg (and with Justice Kagan recusing herself), sharply criticized the reasoning of Justice Kennedy's opinion and the concurring opinions of Chief Justice Roberts and Justice Scalia. Justice Sotomayor countered that Michigan's constitutional amendment barring race-conscious considerations in admissions and other governmental decisions violated the Fourteenth Amendment's Equal Protection Clause, and failed to recognize the persistence of racial bias. Indeed, Justice Sotomayor singled out Chief Justice Roberts's observation, in *Parents Involved in Community Schools v. Seattle School District No. 1*, 551 U.S. 701 (2007) (excerpted in Vol. 2), that "The way to stop discrimination on the basis of race is to stop discriminating on the basis of race." Justice Sotomayor, who grew up in a Bronx housing project and had described herself as "an affirmative action baby" who went on to attend Princeton and Yale Law School, countered that "The way to stop discrimination on the basis of race is to speak openly and candidly on the subject of race, and to apply the Constitution with eyes open to the unfortunate effects of centuries of racial discrimination." And Justice Sotomayor vigorously maintained that "race matters" because of the "long history of racial minorities being denied access to the political process"; the "persistent racial inequality" that remains; and because "of the slights, the snickers, the silent judgments that reinforce the most crippling of thoughts: 'I do not belong here.'" As a result of the decision in *Schuette*, states and localities are free to ban or adopt affirmative-action programs without judicial supervision.

Schuette v. Coalition to Defend Affirmative Action, Integration and Immigrant Rights and Fight for Equality by Any Means Necessary (BAMN)
134 S.Ct. 1623 (2014)

Following the Supreme Court's rulings in *Gratz v. Bollinger*, 539 U.S. 306 (2003) (excerpted in Vol. 2), striking down the University of Michigan's race-conscious undergraduate admissions process that assigned points for various factors, such as race, legacy, and geography; and *Grutter v. Bollinger*, 539 U.S. 306 (2003) (excerpted in Vol. 2), upholding the University of Michigan Law School's "holistic" admissions process, a majority of Michigan voters approved a constitutional amendment barring preferential treatment "on the basis of race, sex, color, ethnicity, or national origin in the operation of public employment, public education, or public contracting." That amendment was challenged by the Coalition to Defend Affirmative Action, Integration and the Immigrant Rights and Fight for Equality by Any Means Necessary (BAMN), among others. A federal district court upheld the amendment, but its decision was reversed by the Court of Appeals for the Sixth Circuit. An appeal of that decision was granted by the Supreme Court.

The appellate court's decision was reversed by a six to two vote (with Justice Kagan recused). Justice Kennedy delivered the opinion for the Court in which only Chief Justice Roberts and Justice Alito joined. Justice Scalia, joined by Justice Thomas, and Justice Breyer issued concurring opinions. Justice Sotomayor, joined by Justice Ginsburg, dissented.

☐ *Justice KENNEDY delivered the opinion of the Court, which THE CHIEF JUSTICE and Justice ALITO joined.*

[I]t is important to note what this case is not about. It is not about the constitutionality, or the merits, of race-conscious admissions policies in higher education. The consideration of race in admissions presents complex questions, in part addressed last Term in *Fisher v. University of Texas at Austin*, [133 S.Ct. 2411] (2013). In *Fisher*, the Court did not disturb the principle that the consideration of race in admissions is permissible, provided that certain conditions are met. In this case, as in *Fisher*, that principle is not challenged. The question here concerns not the permissibility of race-conscious admissions policies under the Constitution but whether, and in what manner, voters in the States may choose to prohibit the consideration of racial preferences in governmental decisions, in particular with respect to school admissions. . . .

[T]his Court's decision in *Reitman v. Mulkey*, 387 U.S. 369 (1967), is a proper beginning point for discussing the controlling decisions. In *Mulkey*, voters amended the California Constitution to prohibit any state legislative interference with an owner's prerogative to decline to sell or rent residential property on any basis [specifically, race]. . . . This Court concluded that the state constitutional provision was a denial of equal protection. . . . The Court agreed that the amendment "expressly authorized and constitutionalized the private right to discriminate." . . .

The next precedent of relevance, *Hunter v. Erickson*, 393 U.S. 385 (1969), is central to the arguments the respondents make in the instant case. In *Hunter*, the Court for the first time elaborated what the Court of Appeals here styled the "political process" doctrine. There, the Akron City Council found that the citizens of Akron consisted of " 'people of different race[s], . . . many of whom live in circumscribed and segregated areas, under sub-standard unhealthful, unsafe, unsanitary and overcrowded conditions, because of discrimination in the sale, lease, rental and financing of housing.' " To address the problem, Akron enacted a fair housing ordinance to prohibit that sort of discrimination. In response, voters amended the city charter to overturn the ordinance and to require that any additional antidiscrimination housing ordinance be approved by referendum. But most other ordinances "regulating the real property market" were not subject to those threshold requirements. The plaintiff, a black woman in Akron, Ohio, alleged that her real estate agent could not show her certain residences because the owners had specified they would not sell to black persons. . . .

Central to the Court's reasoning in *Hunter* was that the charter amendment was enacted in circumstances where widespread racial discrimination in the sale and rental of housing led to segregated housing, forcing many to live in " 'unhealthful, unsafe, unsanitary and overcrowded conditions.' " The Court rejected Akron's flawed "justifications for its discrimination," justifications that by their own terms had the effect of acknowledging the targeted nature of the charter amendment. The Court noted, furthermore, that the charter amendment was unnecessary as a general means of public control over the city council; for the people of Akron already were empowered to overturn ordinances by referendum. The Court found that the city charter amendment, by singling out antidiscrimination ordinances, "places special burden on racial minorities within the governmental process," thus becoming as impermissible as any other government action taken with the invidious intent to injure a racial minority. . . . *Hunter* rests on the unremarkable principle that the State may not alter the procedures of government to target racial minorities. . . .

[*Washington v.*] *Seattle School Dist. No. 1*, [458 U.S. 457 (1982)], is the third case of principal relevance here. There, the school board adopted a mandatory busing program to alleviate racial isolation of minority students in local schools. Voters who opposed the school board's busing plan passed a state initiative that barred busing to desegregate. The Court first determined that, although "white as well as Negro children benefit from" diversity, the school board's plan "inures primarily to the benefit of the minority." The Court next found that "the practical effect" of the state initiative was to "remov[e] the authority to address a racial problem—and only a racial problem—from the existing decisionmaking body, in such a way as to burden minority interests" because advocates of busing "now must seek relief from the state legislature, or from the statewide electorate." The Court therefore found that the initiative had "explicitly us[ed] the racial nature of a decision to determine the decisionmaking process."

Seattle is best understood as a case in which the state action in question (the bar on busing enacted by the State's voters) had the serious risk, if not purpose, of causing specific injuries on account of race, just as had been the case in *Mulkey* and *Hunter*. Although there had been no judicial finding of de jure segregation with respect to Seattle's school district, it appears as though school segregation in the district in the 1940's and 1950's may have been the partial result of school board policies that "permitted white students to transfer out of black schools while restricting the transfer of black students into white schools." *Parents Involved in Community Schools v. Seattle School Dist. No. 1*, 551 U.S. 701–808 (2007) (BREYER, J., dissenting). . . .

As this Court held in *Parents Involved*, the school board's purported remedial action would not be permissible today absent a showing of de jure segregation. That holding prompted Justice BREYER to observe in dissent, as noted above, that one permissible reading of the record was that the school board had maintained policies to perpetuate racial segregation in the schools. In all events we must understand *Seattle* as *Seattle* understood itself, as a case in which neither the State nor the United States "challenge[d] the propriety of race-conscious student assignments for the purpose of achieving integration, even absent a finding of prior de jure segregation." In other words the legitimacy and constitutionality of the remedy in question (busing for desegregation) was assumed, and *Seattle* must be understood on that basis. *Seattle* involved a state initiative that "was carefully tailored to interfere only with desegregative busing." . . .

The broad language used in *Seattle*, however, went well beyond the analysis needed to resolve the case. The Court there seized upon the statement in Justice HARLAN's concurrence in *Hunter* that the procedural change in that case had "the clear purpose of making it more difficult for certain racial and religious minorities to achieve legislation that is in their interest." That language, taken in the context of the facts in *Hunter*, is best read simply to describe the necessity for finding an equal protection violation where specific injuries from hostile discrimination were at issue. The *Seattle* Court, however, used the language from the *Hunter* concurrence to establish a new and far-reaching rationale. *Seattle* stated that where a government policy "inures primarily to the benefit of the minority" and "minorities . . . consider" the policy to be "'in their interest,'" then any state action that "place[s] effective decisionmaking authority over" that policy "at a different level of government" must be reviewed under strict scrutiny. In essence, according to the broad reading of *Seattle*, any state action with a "racial focus" that makes it "more difficult for certain racial minorities than for other groups" to "achieve legislation that is in their interest" is subject to strict scrutiny. It is this reading of *Seattle* that the Court of Appeals found to be controlling here. And that reading must be rejected. . . .

In cautioning against "impermissible racial stereotypes," this Court has rejected the assumption that "members of the same racial group—regardless of their age, education, economic status, or the community in which they live—think alike, share the same political interests, and will prefer the same candidates at the polls." *Shaw v. Reno*, 509 U.S. 630 (1993). It cannot be entertained as a serious proposition that all individuals of the same race think alike. Yet that proposition would be a necessary beginning point were the *Seattle* formulation to control, as the Court of Appeals held it did in this case. And if it were deemed necessary to probe how some races define their own interest in political matters, still another beginning point would be to define individuals according to race. But in a society in which those lines are becoming more blurred, the attempt to define race-based categories also raises serious questions of its own. Government action that classifies individuals on the basis of race is inherently suspect and carries the danger of perpetuating the very racial divisions the polity seeks to transcend. . . .

The freedom secured by the Constitution consists, in one of its essential dimensions, of the right of the individual not to be injured by the unlawful exercise of governmental power. The mandate for segregated schools, *Brown v. Board of Education*, 347 U.S. 483 (1954), and scores of other examples teach that individual liberty has constitutional protection, and that liberty's full extent and meaning may remain yet to be discovered and affirmed. Yet freedom does not stop with individual rights. Our constitutional system embraces, too, the right of citizens to debate so they can learn and decide and then, through the political process, act in concert to try to shape the course of their own times and the course of a nation that must strive always to make freedom ever greater and more secure. Here Michigan voters acted in concert and statewide to seek consensus and adopt a policy on a difficult subject against a historical background of race in America that has been a source of tragedy and persisting injustice. That history demands that we continue to learn, to listen, and to remain open to new approaches if we are to aspire always to a constitutional order in which all persons are treated with fairness and equal dignity. Were the Court to rule that the question addressed by Michigan voters is too sensitive or complex to be within the grasp of the electorate; or that the policies at issue remain too delicate to be resolved save by university officials or faculties, acting at some remove from immediate public scrutiny and control; or that these matters are so arcane that the electorate's power must be limited because the people cannot prudently exercise that power even after a full debate, that holding would be an unprecedented restriction on the exercise of a fundamental right held not just by one person but by all in common. It is the right to speak and debate and learn and then, as a matter of political will, to act through a lawful electoral process.

The respondents in this case insist that a difficult question of public policy must be taken from the reach of the voters, and thus removed from the realm of public discussion, dialogue, and debate in an election campaign. Quite in addition to the serious First Amendment implications of that position with respect to any particular election, it is inconsistent with the underlying premises of a responsible, functioning democracy. One of those premises is that a democracy has the capacity—and the duty—to learn from its past mistakes; to discover and confront persisting biases; and by respectful, rational deliberation to rise above those flaws and injustices. That process is impeded, not advanced, by court decrees based on the proposition that the public cannot have the requisite repose to discuss certain issues. It is demeaning to the democratic process to presume that the voters are not capable of deciding an issue of this sensitivity on decent and rational grounds. The process of public discourse and political debate should not be foreclosed even if there is a risk that during a public campaign there will be those, on both sides, who seek to use racial division and discord to their own political advantage. An informed public can, and must, rise above this. The idea of democracy is that it can, and must, mature. Freedom embraces the right, indeed the duty, to engage in a rational, civic discourse in order to determine how best to form a consensus to shape the destiny of the Nation and its people. These First Amendment dynamics would be disserved if this Court were to say that the question here at issue is beyond the capacity of the voters to debate and then to determine. . . .

This case is not about how the debate about racial preferences should be resolved. It is about who may resolve it. There is no authority in the Constitution of the United States or in this Court's precedents for the Judiciary to set aside Michigan laws that commit this policy determination to the voters. Deliberative debate on sensitive issues such as racial preferences all too often may shade into rancor. But that does not justify removing certain court-determined issues from the voters' reach. Democracy does not presume that some subjects are either too divisive or too profound for public debate.

☐ *CHIEF JUSTICE ROBERTS, concurring.*

The dissent states that "[t]he way to stop discrimination on the basis of race is to speak openly and candidly on the subject of race." And it urges that "[r]ace matters because of the slights, the snickers, the silent judgments that reinforce that most crippling of thoughts: 'I do not belong here.'" But it is not "out of touch with reality" to conclude that racial preferences may themselves have the debilitating effect of reinforcing precisely that doubt, and—if so—that the preferences do more harm than good. To disagree with the dissent's views on the costs and benefits of racial preferences is not to "wish away, rather than confront" racial inequality. People can disagree in good faith on this issue, but it similarly does more harm than good to question the openness and candor of those on either side of the debate.

☐ *Justice SCALIA, with whom Justice THOMAS joins, concurring in the judgment.*

It has come to this. Called upon to explore the jurisprudential twilight zone between two errant lines of precedent, we confront a frighteningly bizarre question: Does the Equal Protection Clause of the Fourteenth Amendment forbid what its text plainly requires? Needless to say (except that this case obliges us to say it), the question answers itself. "The Constitution proscribes government discrimination on the basis of race, and state-provided education is no exception." *Grutter v. Bollinger* (SCALIA, J., concurring in part and dissenting in part). It is precisely this understanding—the correct understanding—of the federal Equal Protection Clause that the people of the State of

Michigan have adopted for their own fundamental law. By adopting it, they did not simultaneously offend it.

Even taking this Court's sorry line of race-based-admissions cases as a given, I find the question presented only slightly less strange: Does the Equal Protection Clause forbid a State from banning a practice that the Clause barely—and only provisionally—permits? Reacting to those race-based-admissions decisions, some States—whether deterred by the prospect of costly litigation; aware that *Grutter's* bell may soon toll, or simply opposed in principle to the notion of "benign" racial discrimination—have gotten out of the racial-preferences business altogether. And with our express encouragement: "Universities in California, Florida, and Washington State, where racial preferences in admissions are prohibited by state law, are currently engaging in experimenting with a wide variety of alternative approaches. Universities in other States can and should draw on the most promising aspects of these race-neutral alternatives as they develop." Respondents seem to think this admonition was merely in jest. The experiment, they maintain, is not only over; it never rightly began. Neither the people of the States nor their legislatures ever had the option of directing subordinate public-university officials to cease considering the race of applicants, since that would deny members of those minority groups the option of enacting a policy designed to further their interest, thus denying them the equal protection of the laws. Never mind that it is hotly disputed whether the practice of race-based admissions is ever in a racial minority's interest. And never mind that, were a public university to stake its defense of a race-based-admissions policy on the ground that it was designed to benefit primarily minorities (as opposed to all students, regardless of color, by enhancing diversity), we would hold the policy unconstitutional.

But the battleground for this case is not the constitutionality of race-based admissions—at least, not quite. Rather, it is the so-called political-process doctrine, derived from this Court's opinions in *Washington v. Seattle School Dist. No. 1* and *Hunter v. Erickson*. I agree with those parts of the plurality opinion that repudiate this doctrine. But I do not agree with its reinterpretation of *Seattle* and *Hunter*, which makes them stand in part for the cloudy and doctrinally anomalous proposition that whenever state action poses "the serious risk . . . of causing specific injuries on account of race," it denies equal protection. I would instead reaffirm that the "ordinary principles of our law [and] of our democratic heritage" require "plaintiffs alleging equal protection violations" stemming from facially neutral acts to "prove intent and causation and not merely the existence of racial disparity." *Freeman v. Pitts*, 503 U.S. 467 (1992) (SCALIA, J., concurring). . . .

Patently atextual, unadministrable, and contrary to our traditional equal-protection jurisprudence, *Hunter* and *Seattle* should be overruled. . . .

The dissent trots out the old saw, derived from dictum in a footnote, that legislation motivated by "'prejudice against discrete and insular minorities'" merits "'more exacting judicial scrutiny.'" (quoting *United States v. Carolene Products*, 304 U.S. 144–153, n. 4). I say derived from that dictum (expressed by the four-Justice majority of a seven-Justice Court) because the dictum itself merely said "[n]or need we enquire . . . whether prejudice against discrete and insular minorities may be a special condition." The dissent does not argue, of course, that such "prejudice" produced Section 26. Nor does it explain why certain racial minorities in Michigan qualify as "'insular,'" meaning that "other groups will not form coalitions with them—and, critically, not because of lack of common interests but because of 'prejudice.'" . . . But the more important point is that we should not design our jurisprudence to conform to dictum in a footnote in a four-Justice opinion. . . .

As Justice HARLAN observed over a century ago, "[o]ur Constitution is color-blind, and neither knows nor tolerates classes among citizens." *Plessy v. Ferguson*, 163 U.S. 537 (1896) (dissenting opinion). The people of Michigan wish the same for their governing charter. It would be shameful for us to stand in their way.

[Justice BREYER concurred in the judgment because (1) Michigan universities considered race in admission not for the reason of remedying past discrimination but for the less significant reason of promoting diverse student bodies and (2) the constitutional amendment transferred authority to make decisions about affirmative action from "unelected faculty members and administrators" to the voters themselves, and thus reinforced participatory democracy.]

☐ *Justice SOTOMAYOR, with whom Justice GINSBURG joins, dissenting.*

We are fortunate to live in a democratic society. But without checks, democratically approved legislation can oppress minority groups. For that reason, our Constitution places limits on what a majority of the people may do. This case implicates one such limit: the guarantee of equal protection of the laws. Although that guarantee is traditionally understood to prohibit intentional discrimination under existing laws, equal protection does not end there. Another fundamental strand of our equal protection jurisprudence focuses on process, securing to all citizens the right to participate meaningfully and equally in self-government. That right is the bedrock of our democracy, for it preserves all other rights.

Yet to know the history of our Nation is to understand its long and lamentable record of stymieing the right of racial minorities to participate in the political process. At first, the majority acted with an open, invidious purpose. Notwithstanding the command of the Fifteenth Amendment, certain States shut racial minorities out of the political process altogether by withholding the right to vote. This Court intervened to preserve that right. The majority tried again, replacing outright bans on voting with literacy tests, good character requirements, poll taxes, and gerrymandering. The Court was not fooled; it invalidated those measures, too. The majority persisted. This time, although it allowed the minority access to the political process, the majority changed the ground rules of the process so as to make it more difficult for the minority, and the minority alone, to obtain policies designed to foster racial integration. Although these political restructurings may not have been discriminatory in purpose, the Court reaffirmed the right of minority members of our society to participate meaningfully and equally in the political process.

This case involves this last chapter of discrimination: A majority of the Michigan electorate changed the basic rules of the political process in that State in a manner that uniquely disadvantaged racial minorities. . . .

As a result of Section 26, there are now two very different processes through which a Michigan citizen is permitted to influence the admissions policies of the State's universities: one for persons interested in race-sensitive admissions policies and one for everyone else. A citizen who is a University of Michigan alumnus, for instance, can advocate for an admissions policy that considers an applicant's legacy status by meeting individually with members of the Board of Regents to convince them of her views, by joining with other legacy parents to lobby the Board, or by voting for and supporting Board candidates who share her position. The same options are available to a citizen who wants the Board to adopt admissions policies that consider athleticism, geography, area of study, and so on. The one and only policy a Michigan citizen may not seek through this long-established process is a race-sensitive admissions policy that considers race in an individualized manner when it is clear that race-neutral alternatives are not adequate to achieve diversity. For that policy alone, the citizens of Michigan must undertake the daunting task of amending the State Constitution.

Our precedents do not permit political restructurings that create one process for racial minorities and a separate, less burdensome process for everyone else. This Court has held that the Fourteenth Amendment does not tolerate "a political structure that treats all individuals as equals, yet more subtly distorts governmental processes in such a way as to place special burdens on the ability of minority groups to achieve beneficial legislation." *Washington v. Seattle School Dist. No. 1*, 458 U.S. 457 (1982). Such restructuring, the Court explained, "is no more permissible than denying [the minority] the [right to] vote, on an equal basis with others." *Hunter.* In those cases—*Hunter* and *Seattle*—the Court recognized what is now known as the "political-process doctrine": When the majority reconfigures the political process in a manner that burdens only a racial minority, that alteration triggers strict judicial scrutiny.

Today, disregarding *stare decisis*, a majority of the Court effectively discards those precedents. . . .

The plurality's decision fundamentally misunderstands the nature of the injustice worked by Section 26. . . . I firmly believe that our role as judges includes policing the process of self-government and stepping in when necessary to secure the constitutional guarantee of equal protection. Because I would do so here, I respectfully dissent.

For much of its history, our Nation has denied to many of its citizens the right to participate meaningfully and equally in its politics. This is a history we strive to put behind us. But it is a history that still informs the society we live in, and so it is one we must address with candor. Because the political-process doctrine is best understood against the backdrop of this history, I will briefly trace its course.

The Fifteenth Amendment, ratified after the Civil War, promised to racial minorities the right to vote. But many States ignored this promise. In addition to outright tactics of fraud, intimidation, and violence, there are countless examples of States categorically denying to racial minorities access to the political process. . . .

Some States were less direct. Oklahoma was one of many that required all voters to pass a literacy test. But the test did not apply equally to all voters. Under a "grandfather clause," voters were exempt if their grand-fathers had been voters or had served as soldiers before 1866. This meant, of course, that black voters had to pass the test, but many white voters did not. The Court held the scheme unconstitutional. *Guinn v. United States*, 238 U.S. 347 (1915). In response, Oklahoma changed the rules. It enacted a new statute under which all voters who were qualified to vote in 1914 (under the unconstitutional grandfather clause) remained qualified, and the remaining voters had to apply for registration within a 12-day period. *Lane v. Wilson*, 307 U.S. 268–271 (1939). The Court struck down that statute as well. . . .

This Court's landmark ruling in *Brown v. Board of Education* (1954) triggered a new era of political restructuring, this time in the context of education.

In Virginia, the General Assembly transferred control of student assignment from local school districts to a State Pupil Placement Board. And when the legislature learned that the Arlington County school board had prepared a desegregation plan, the General Assembly "swiftly retaliated" by stripping the county of its right to elect its school board by popular vote and instead making the board an appointed body.

The Court remained true to its command in *Brown*. In Arkansas, for example, it enforced a desegregation order against the Little Rock school board. *Cooper v. Aaron*, 358 U.S. 1 (1958). On the very day the Court announced that ruling, the Arkansas Legislature responded by changing the rules. It enacted a law permitting the Governor to close any public school in the State, and stripping local school districts of their decisionmaking authority so long as the Governor determined that local officials could not maintain "'a general, suitable, and efficient educational system.'"

The States' political restructuring efforts in the 1960's and 1970's went beyond the context of education. Many States tried to suppress the political voice of racial minorities more generally by reconfiguring the manner in which they filled vacancies in local offices, often transferring authority from the electorate (where minority citizens had a voice at the local level) to the States' executive branch (where minorities wielded little if any influence).

It was in this historical context that the Court intervened in *Hunter v. Erickson*, 393 U.S. 385 (1969), and *Washington v. Seattle School Dist. No. 1*, 458 U.S. 457 (1982). Together, *Hunter* and *Seattle* recognized a fundamental strand of this Court's equal protection jurisprudence: the political-process doctrine. . . .

Before the enactment of Section 26, Michigan's political structure permitted both supporters and opponents of race-sensitive admissions policies to vote for their candidates of choice and to lobby the elected and politically accountable boards. Section 26 reconfigured that structure. After Section 26, the boards retain plenary authority over all admissions criteria except for race-sensitive admissions policies. To change admissions policies on this one issue, a Michigan citizen must instead amend the Michigan Constitution. That is no small task. To place a proposed constitutional amendment on the ballot requires either the support of two-thirds of both Houses of the Michigan Legislature or a vast number of signatures from Michigan voters—10 percent of the total number of votes cast in the preceding gubernatorial election. Since more than 3.2 million votes were cast in the 2010 election for Governor, more than 320,000 signatures are currently needed to win a ballot spot. . . . And the costs of qualifying an amendment are significant. . . .

It is nothing short of baffling . . . for the plurality to insist—in the face of clear language in *Hunter* and *Seattle* saying otherwise—that those cases were about nothing more than the intentional and invidious infliction of a racial injury. The plurality's attempt to rewrite *Hunter* and *Seattle* so as to cast aside the political-process doctrine *sub silentio* is impermissible as a matter of *stare decisis*. Under the doctrine of *stare decisis*, we usually stand by our decisions, even if we disagree with them, because people rely on what we say, and they believe they can take us at our word.

And what now of the political-process doctrine? After the plurality's revision of *Hunter* and *Seattle*, it is unclear what is left. The plurality certainly does not tell us. On this point, and this point only, I agree with Justice SCALIA that the plurality has rewritten those precedents beyond recognition.

Justice BREYER concludes that *Hunter* and *Seattle* do not apply. Section 26, he reasons, did not move the relevant decisionmaking authority from one political level to another; rather, it removed that authority from "unelected actors and placed it in the hands of the voters." He bases this conclusion on the premise that Michigan's elected boards "delegated admissions-related decision-making authority to unelected university faculty members and administrators." But this premise is simply incorrect.

For one thing, it is undeniable that prior to Section 26, board candidates often pledged to end or carry on the use of race-sensitive admissions policies at Michigan's public universities. Surely those were not empty promises. Indeed, the issue of race-sensitive admissions policies often dominated board elections. . . . The boards retain ultimate authority to adopt or reject admissions policies in at least three ways. First, they routinely meet with university officials to review admissions policies, including race-sensitive admissions policies. . . . Second, the boards may enact bylaws with respect to specific admissions policies and may alter any admissions policies set by university officials. . . . Finally, the boards may appoint university officials who share their admissions goals, and they may remove those officials if the officials' goals diverge from those of the boards. . . .

The salient point is this: Although the elected and politically accountable boards may well entrust university officials with certain day-to-day admissions responsibilities, they often weigh in on admissions policies themselves and, at all times, they retain complete supervisory authority over university officials and overall admissions decisions. . . .

The political-process doctrine not only resolves this case as a matter of *stare decisis*; it is correct as a matter of first principles.

Under our Constitution, majority rule is not without limit. Our system of government is predicated on an equilibrium between the notion that a majority of citizens may determine governmental policy through legislation enacted by their elected representatives, and the overriding principle that there are nonetheless some things the Constitution forbids even a majority of citizens to do. The political-process doctrine, grounded in the Fourteenth Amendment, is a central check on majority rule. . . .

Few rights are as fundamental as the right to participate meaningfully and equally in the process of government. See *Yick Wo v. Hopkins*, 118 U.S. 356 (1886) (political rights are "fundamental" because they are "preservative of all rights"). That right is the bedrock of our democracy, recognized from its very inception. . . .

This right was hardly novel at the time of *Hunter* and *Seattle*. For example, this Court focused on the vital importance of safeguarding minority groups' access to the political process in *United States v. Carolene Products Co.*, 304 U.S. 144 (1938), a case that predated *Hunter* by 30 years. In a now-famous footnote, the Court explained that while ordinary social and economic legislation carries a presumption of constitutionality, the same may not be true of legislation that offends fundamental rights or targets minority groups. Citing cases involving restrictions on the right to vote, restraints on the dissemination of information, interferences with political organizations, and prohibition of peaceable assembly, the Court recognized that "legislation which restricts those political processes which can ordinarily be expected to bring about repeal of undesirable legislation" could be worthy of "more exacting judicial scrutiny under the general prohibitions of the Fourteenth Amendment than are most other types of legislation." The Court also noted that "prejudice against discrete and insular minorities may be a special condition, which tends seriously to curtail the operation of those political processes ordinarily to be relied upon to protect minorities, and which may call for a correspondingly more searching judicial inquiry. . . .

Our cases recognize at least three features of the right to meaningful participation in the political process. Two of them, thankfully, are uncontroversial.

First, every eligible citizen has a right to vote. This, woefully, has not always been the case. But it is a right no one would take issue with today. Second, the majority may not make it more difficult for the minority to exercise the right to vote. This, too, is widely accepted. After all, the Court has invalidated grandfather clauses, good character requirements, poll taxes, and gerrymandering provisions. The third feature, the one the plurality dismantles today, is that a majority may not reconfigure the existing political process in a manner that creates a two-tiered system of political change, subjecting laws designed to protect or benefit discrete and insular minorities to a more burdensome political process than all other laws. This is the political-process doctrine of *Hunter* and *Seattle*.

My colleagues would stop at the second. The plurality embraces the freedom of "self-government" without limits. And Justice SCALIA values a "near-limitless" notion of state sovereignty. The wrong sought to be corrected by the political-process doctrine, they say, is not one that should concern us and is in any event beyond the reach of the Fourteenth Amendment. As they see it, the Court's role in protecting the political process ends once we have removed certain barriers to the minority's participation in that process. Then, they say, we must sit back and let the majority rule without the key constitutional limit recognized in *Hunter* and *Seattle*.

That view drains the Fourteenth Amendment of one of its core teachings. Contrary to today's decision, protecting the right to meaningful participation in the political process must mean more than simply removing barriers to participation. It must mean vigilantly policing the political process to ensure that the majority does not use other methods to prevent minority groups from partaking in that process on equal footing. Why? For the same reason we guard the right of every citizen to vote. . . .

To accept the first two features of the right to meaningful participation in the political process, while renouncing the third, paves the way for the majority to do what it has done time and again throughout our Nation's history: afford the minority the opportunity to participate, yet manipulate the ground rules so as to ensure the minority's defeat. This is entirely at odds with our idea of equality under the law. . . .

To reiterate, none of this is to say that the political-process doctrine prohibits the exercise of democratic self-government. Nothing prevents a majority of citizens from pursuing or obtaining its preferred outcome in a political contest. Here, for instance, I agree with the plurality that Michiganders who were unhappy with *Grutter* were free to pursue an end to race-sensitive admissions policies in their State. They were free to elect governing boards that opposed race-sensitive admissions policies or, through public discourse and dialogue, to lobby the existing boards toward that end. They were also free to remove from the boards the authority to make any decisions with respect to admissions policies, as opposed to only decisions concerning race-sensitive admissions policies. But what the majority could not do, consistent with the Constitution, is change the ground rules of the political process in a manner that makes it more difficult for racial minorities alone to achieve their goals. In doing so, the majority effectively rigs the contest to guarantee a particular outcome. That is the very wrong the political-process doctrine seeks to remedy. The doctrine "hews to the unremarkable notion that when two competitors are running a race, one may not require the other to run twice as far or to scale obstacles not present in the first runner's course." . . .

My colleagues are of the view that we should leave race out of the picture entirely and let the voters sort it out. We have seen this reasoning before. See

Parents Involved ("The way to stop discrimination on the basis of race is to stop discriminating on the basis of race"). It is a sentiment out of touch with reality, one not required by our Constitution, and one that has properly been rejected as "not sufficient" to resolve cases of this nature. While "[t]he enduring hope is that race should not matter[,] the reality is that too often it does." "[R]acial discrimination . . . [is] not ancient history." *Bartlett v. Strickland*, 556 U.S. 1 (2009) (plurality opinion).

Race matters. Race matters in part because of the long history of racial minorities' being denied access to the political process.

Race also matters because of persistent racial inequality in society—inequality that cannot be ignored and that has produced stark socioeconomic disparities.

And race matters for reasons that really are only skin deep, that cannot be discussed any other way, and that cannot be wished away. Race matters to a young man's view of society when he spends his teenage years watching others tense up as he passes, no matter the neighborhood where he grew up. Race matters to a young woman's sense of self when she states her hometown, and then is pressed, "No, where are you really from?", regardless of how many generations her family has been in the country. Race matters to a young person addressed by a stranger in a foreign language, which he does not understand because only English was spoken at home. Race matters because of the slights, the snickers, the silent judgments that reinforce that most crippling of thoughts: "I do not belong here."

In my colleagues' view, examining the racial impact of legislation only perpetuates racial discrimination. This refusal to accept the stark reality that race matters is regrettable. The way to stop discrimination on the basis of race is to speak openly and candidly on the subject of race, and to apply the Constitution with eyes open to the unfortunate effects of centuries of racial discrimination. As members of the judiciary tasked with intervening to carry out the guarantee of equal protection, we ought not sit back and wish away, rather than confront, the racial inequality that exists in our society. It is this view that works harm, by perpetuating the facile notion that what makes race matter is acknowledging the simple truth that race does matter.

Although the only constitutional rights at stake in this case are process-based rights, the substantive policy at issue is undeniably of some relevance to my colleagues. I will therefore speak in response.

For over a century, racial minorities in Michigan fought to bring diversity to their State's public colleges and universities. Before the advent of race-sensitive admissions policies, those institutions, like others around the country, were essentially segregated. In 1868, two black students were admitted to the University of Michigan, the first of their race. In 1935, over six decades later, there were still only 35 black students at the University. By 1954, this number had risen to slightly below 200. And by 1966, to around 400, among a total student population of roughly 32,500—barely over 1 percent. The numbers at the University of Michigan Law School are even more telling. During the 1960's, the Law School produced 9 black graduates among a total of 3,041—less than three-tenths of 1 percent. . . .

During the 1970's, the University continued to improve its admissions policies, encouraged by this Court's 1978 decision in [*Regents of the University of California v.*] *Bakke* [438 U.S. 265 (1978)]. In that case, the Court told our Nation's colleges and universities that they could consider race in admissions as part of a broader goal to create a diverse student body, in which students of different backgrounds would learn together, and thereby learn to live together.

A little more than a decade ago, in *Grutter*, the Court reaffirmed this understanding. In upholding the admissions policy of the Law School, the Court laid to rest any doubt whether student body diversity is a compelling interest that may justify the use of race.

Race-sensitive admissions policies are now a thing of the past in Michigan after Section 26, even though—as experts agree and as research shows—those policies were making a difference in achieving educational diversity. . . .

Section 26 has already led to decreased minority enrollment at Michigan's public colleges and universities. In 2006 (before Section 26 took effect), underrepresented minorities made up 12.15 percent of the University of Michigan's freshman class, compared to 9.54 percent in 2012—a roughly 25 percent decline. Moreover, the total number of college-aged underrepresented minorities in Michigan has increased even as the number of underrepresented minorities admitted to the University has decreased. For example, between 2006 and 2011, the proportion of black freshmen among those enrolled at the University of Michigan declined from 7 percent to 5 percent, even though the proportion of black college-aged persons in Michigan increased from 16 to 19 percent. . . .

The President and Chancellors of the University of California (which has 10 campuses, not 17) inform us that "[t]he abandonment of race-conscious admissions policies resulted in an immediate and precipitous decline in the rates at which underrepresented-minority students applied to, were admitted to, and enrolled at" the university. *Brief for President and Chancellors of the University of California as Amici Curiae.* At the University of California, Los Angeles (UCLA), for example, admission rates for underrepresented minorities plummeted from 52.4 percent in 1995 (before California's ban took effect) to 24 percent in 1998. As a result, the percentage of underrepresented minorities fell by more than half: from 30.1 percent of the entering class in 1995 to 14.3 percent in 1998. The admissions rate for underrepresented minorities at UCLA reached a new low of 13.6 percent in 2012.

The elimination of race-sensitive admissions policies in California has been especially harmful to black students. In 2006, for example, there were fewer than 100 black students in UCLA's incoming class of roughly 5,000, the lowest number since at least 1973. . . .

As in Michigan, the declines in minority representation at the University of California have come even as the minority population in California has increased. At UCLA, for example, the proportion of Hispanic freshmen among those enrolled declined from 23 percent in 1995 to 17 percent in 2011, even though the proportion of Hispanic college-aged persons in California increased from 41 percent to 49 percent during that same period. . . .

These statistics may not influence the views of some of my colleagues, as they question the wisdom of adopting race-sensitive admissions policies and would prefer if our Nation's colleges and universities were to discard those policies altogether. (ROBERTS, C. J., concurring) (suggesting that race-sensitive admissions policies might "do more harm than good"); (SCALIA, J., concurring in judgment); *Grutter* (THOMAS, J., concurring in part and dissenting in part). That view is at odds with our recognition in *Grutter*, and more recently in *Fisher v. University of Texas at Austin* that race-sensitive admissions policies are necessary to achieve a diverse student body when race-neutral alternatives have failed. More fundamentally, it ignores the importance of diversity in institutions of higher education and reveals how little my colleagues understand about the reality of race in America. . . .

Colleges and universities must be free to prioritize the goal of diversity. They must be free to immerse their students in a multiracial environment that fosters frequent and meaningful interactions with students of other races, and thereby pushes such students to transcend any assumptions they may hold on the basis of skin color. Without race-sensitive admissions policies, this might well be impossible. The statistics I have described make that fact glaringly obvious. We should not turn a blind eye to something we cannot help but see. . . .

I cannot ignore the unfortunate outcome of today's decision: Short of amending the State Constitution, a Herculean task, racial minorities in Michigan are deprived of even an opportunity to convince Michigan's public colleges and universities to consider race in their admissions plans when other attempts to achieve racial diversity have proved unworkable, and those institutions are unnecessarily hobbled in their pursuit of a diverse student body.

The Constitution does not protect racial minorities from political defeat. But neither does it give the majority free rein to erect selective barriers against racial minorities. The political-process doctrine polices the channels of change to ensure that the majority, when it wins, does so without rigging the rules of the game to ensure its success. Today, the Court discards that doctrine without good reason.

In doing so, it permits the decision of a majority of the voters in Michigan to strip Michigan's elected university boards of their authority to make decisions with respect to constitutionally permissible race-sensitive admissions policies, while preserving the boards' plenary authority to make all other educational decisions. The Court abdicates [its] role, permitting the majority to use its numerical advantage to change the rules mid-contest and forever stack the deck against racial minorities in Michigan. The result is that Michigan's public colleges and universities are less equipped to do their part in ensuring that students of all races are "better prepare[d] . . . for an increasingly diverse workforce and society. . . ." *Grutter*.

Today's decision eviscerates an important strand of our equal protection jurisprudence. For members of historically marginalized groups, which rely on the federal courts to protect their constitutional rights, the decision can hardly bolster hope for a vision of democracy that preserves for all the right to participate meaningfully and equally in self-government.

I respectfully dissent.

INDEX OF CASES

Cases printed in boldface are excerpted on the page(s) printed in boldface.

Other Books by David M. O'Brien

Storm Center:
The Supreme Court in American Politics
10th ed.

Constitutional Law and Politics:
Vol. 1. *Struggles for Power and Governmental Accountability*
Vol. 2. *Civil Rights and Civil Liberties*
9th ed.

Congress Shall Make No Law: The First Amendment,
Unprotected Expression, and the U.S. Supreme Court

Animal Sacrifice and Religious Freedom:
Church of Lukumi Babalu Aye v. City of Hialeah

To Dream of Dreams:
Religious Freedom and Constitutional Politics in Postwar Japan

Judicial Roulette

What Process Is Due?
Courts and Science-Policy Disputes

The Public's Right to Know:
The Supreme Court and the First Amendment

Privacy, Law, and Public Policy

Judges on Judging: Views from the Bench
4th ed. (editor)

The Lanahan Readings on Civil Rights and Civil Liberties
3rd ed. (editor)

Abortion and American Politics
(co-author)

Judicial Independence in the Age of Democracy:
Critical Perspectives from Around the World
(co-editor)

The Politics of Technology Assessment:
Institutions, Processes, and Policy Disputes
(co-editor)

Views from the Bench:
The Judiciary and Constitutional Politics
(co-editor)

The Politics of American Government
3rd ed. (co-author)

Government by the People
22nd ed. (co-author)

Courts and Judicial Policymaking
(co-author)